MICRO

BUSINE

In the same series
The Electronic Calculator in Business, Home and School
Your Business, The Right Way to Run It

MICRO-COMPUTERS

FOR

BUSINESS AND HOME

by
A. D. T. FRYER

PAPERFRONTS
ELLIOT RIGHT WAY BOOKS
KINGSWOOD SURREY UK

Made and Printed in Great Britain by
Cox and Wyman, Reading.

CONTENTS

LIST OF ILLUSTRATIONS

To my parents
and
my wife Margaret and daughter Helen

Acknowledgements

Thanks are due to the following firms for demonstrations of the programs described in chapter 4.

J. K. Greye Software Ltd., of Bath
Compsoft Ltd., of Shamley Green near Guildford
KGB Micros Ltd., of Slough
Graffcom Systems Ltd., of London
Comshare Ltd. (Micro Products Division), of London
Hilderbay Ltd., of London

Special thanks are due to the author's employers, Micro Focus Ltd., of London, Swindon and Santa Clara (California), for encouragement and facilities.

1
INTRODUCTION

1. Intentions of the book

This book is intended for someone who knows nothing about computers, and is wondering if one would be useful. It is written for the owner of a small business, or a householder, but should be of equal interest to someone thinking of using a computer as a hobby, or in some specialised field such as a school or a doctor's practice.

For brevity the word "computer" is used throughout, but this book is only about micro-computers, or personal computers, the small, one-man operated computers costing between say £50 and £5000. This is a wide range of machines, and constant improvements in the designs of new computers make it even wider. Nevertheless the basic purpose and design of all computers is the same, and so one book can cover this range with only a few asides to point out differences.

Computers are a subject people can understand to different depths. You can, for example, use a computer successfully for many years while hardly hearing of programming. The seven chapters are designed to enable you to read as far as you choose. Different chapters do not cover different parts of the subject, but rather go into it in successively greater depth. You can stop reading at the end of any chapter, perhaps to continue later with the next chapter if you decide to go deeper. There are also a few places where you can choose to read only one or two of several alternative sections depending on your interests.

The intention of the chapters is as follows:
1. To explain where and how to buy a computer.
2. To enable you to follow when a computer is being demonstrated to you in a shop.

3. To point out what you should know to buy and use a computer.
4. To show examples of what you can use a computer for.
5. To show what programming is like.
6. To explain programming in detail.
7. To show how you write a program.

At the first reading you should read the book from the beginning, as most chapters use words explained earlier. However, each chapter is divided up into short sections so you can subsequently refer back to it easily. Wherever a technical term is used for the first time it is printed in italics and explained.

2. Buying a computer

Buying a computer is rather like buying a hi-fi, in that there are several units that you choose separately and plug into one another, though usually from the same manufacturer's range.

After reading this book, or the chapters you require, you should buy several of the computer magazines to be found in most newsagents. The advertisements in these give a virtually complete view of what is available, and since new products appear and prices drop almost every month will give up-to-date details that no book can. Most of the magazines are written with consideration for the newcomer, but obviously they cannot explain every term in every issue.

Some of the best known magazines are:

Micro Decision	– for business
Your Computer	– mainly for hobbyists
Practical Computing	– for all micro-computer users
Personal Computer World	– for all micro-computer users
Computing Today	– for all micro-computer users
Popular Computing Weekly	– for hobbyists
Which Micro?	– for all micro-computer users
Byte	– American, for all micro-computer users.

Most purchases start with these advertisements. Computers intended for home or hobby use are sold mainly by mail order, though they are appearing in large stationers' and electrical appliance shops too. Generally they cost between

£50 and £1000. Computers intended for business are advertised by the manufacturer or, more usually, a dealer, and it is usually best to ring to arrange to see it demonstrated; many have small staffs, and a demonstration may take several hours. On a business computer you would probably spend between £500 and £5000. Many computers, though, are suitable for both home and business.

There are also specialist computer shops. Some concentrate on computers for business and other serious use, some on computers for the home, and some on equipment for electronics enthusiasts who want to build their own. Here too it is best to have worked out in advance, from their advertisements in magazines, roughly what you want, and often best to ring before going.

A computer is, above all, a machine for storing information, and the total price you pay will depend to a great extent on the type and capacity of units you choose for storing information. Apart from this the cheaper computers are often the simplest to use, because they are intended for the home user.

You can get a lot of useful advice, both before and after buying a computer, by joining a user group. A user group is a club for users of a particular make of computer. They vary a lot, some being clubs for enthusiasts, some being pressure groups formed by business people to keep in touch with the manufacturers.

2
UNDERSTANDING A DEMONSTRATION

1. Some common terms

In any speciality there are some commonly used terms that, though their meanings are simple, may mystify the newcomer because they are unfamiliar. There are also some terms whose use may require comment. Some of the commonest are given here.

Character A single symbol, such as a letter of the alphabet, a digit or a punctuation mark.

Computer The term is misleading. In most uses performing calculations is only part of a computer's main task of storing information.

Data Means "information". This is why in computing people say "data is" whereas in other fields people use the word as a plural.

Device A computer has several distinct parts. These are called "devices".

Machine People very often refer to a computer simply as "the machine".

2. What a computer is for

FILES

A computer is a machine for storing information. You keep information on a computer in *files*. These are much the same as if they were written in ledger books. A business will have a file for each purpose, for example an employee file, a customer file etc., containing one entry for each employee, customer or whatever. An entry is called a *record*. Each item of information in a record, for example an employee's name, date of birth etc., is called a *field*.

The files are recorded on tape cassettes or something very similar called *discs*. The computer records them in a form suitable for it to handle; if you listened to a cassette on a tape recorder you'd hear only bleeps. You use the computer to read, update and set up files.

A computer has a screen, like a television screen. It is intended for displaying text, so you can see information in a record. There is a keyboard, like a typewriter's, so you can add information.

PROGRAMS

One computer can be used for many different jobs. For each job you want your computer to do you have a *program*; without a program a computer will do nothing at all. (Note the spelling; just as French terms are used in cooking, in computing American usages are often preferred. "Program" is almost always spelt without a final "me".)

A computer has a repertoire of operations it can carry out on the data in your files; operations such as adding one number to another, inserting a new record, displaying part of a record on the screen, and so on. Each operation has a number, called an *instruction*, and you can describe some long and complicated action to be done on a file by composing a sequence of these instructions. This is a program. You keep this recorded on tape or disc too; it's called a *program file*. You can make the computer *execute*, or *run*, any program on file whenever you wish; the computer goes through it carrying out each instruction in turn.

To write a short program, of a few instructions, is simple. But many programs consist of hundreds or even thousands of instructions, so most people prefer to buy ready-written programs; there are programs available for most common uses, or *applications*. Programs are often called *software*, while a computer and any ancillary equipment are called *hardware*. A firm that produces programs for sale is called a *software house*. You buy programs recorded on tape or disc.

A program is written for a particular make of computer, or group of makes, and you must make sure your computer is suitable for a program you want to buy. Chapter 3 goes into details. Beyond that most of what was said about buying computers is also true of buying programs. You generally find what you want through advertisements in magazines, and buy by mail order, or for a business program by ringing and arranging a demonstration of what the program does. Programs for the home generally cost between £2 and £50, programs for business between say £20 and £1000; many business programs are around £300. There are even user groups for some of the best known programs.

OTHER WAYS OF USING A COMPUTER

A computer's screen can display pictures as well as text; also, a file can contain data describing pictures, and you can use the keyboard to make pictures on the screen move around. So a computer can equally well be used for graphs, diagrams, and (very common in home computing) video games.

You can also have programs with which you use the computer like a calculator, to display on the screen answers to calculations you type in.

A computer can be connected to electrical machinery. With a program running that measures and controls voltages it can control the machinery. This is called *process control*. It is unlikely to be of interest in a home or small business, because connecting the machinery might mean considerable rewiring of your premises, and because the program would probably have to be specially written.

DATA IN PROGRAMS

Some standard data, rather than being stored in a separate data file, may be stored in the program file. In a business program, for example, the level of income at which each tax band starts may be written into the program like this. If these amounts should change because of changes in the law, the dealer or software house may send you an updated version of the program.

On some small computers there is no facility for storing data files at all. All data is stored in the same file as the program that works on it. Every time you run a program, if the data stored is to be altered the program records an updated version of itself on the tape or disc.

PROCESSING FILES

When you have information in a file there are usually several things you want to do to it.

1. *Update* it, that is add or delete records or change details in a record.
2. Look up information.
3. Get lists of information.

In cases 2 and 3 you may want information that is not actually in the file but can be worked out from information that is.

Generally, for each file you have you will have a program or set of programs, called a *suite* or *system*, to enable you to do these things. Doing anything to a file, or to any data, is called *processing* it. Keeping a file up to date, looking up information and getting lists of information, is called *maintaining* it.

As well as the file it is intended to maintain, a program or suite may maintain some smaller files in which it stores data necessary for its internal working. The user scarcely need be aware of these. They are called *work files*, and the main file is called the *master file*.

When a program reads data from a file, the file is called an *input file* of that program. If a program creates a file the file is called an *output file* of the program.

When you buy a program or suite you are in effect buying the facility to keep a particular master file. Thus you buy a payroll suite if you want to keep a payroll file, a stock control suite for a stock levels file, and so on. What information you keep in a file, and in what form you get information in and out, depends on the program or suite. You should therefore take great care in buying a program or suite that it gives you the facilities you need.

TYPES OF PROGRAM

Suites on the market for file maintenance vary greatly, but a typical one includes an *update program*, an *enquiry program* and several *report programs*. With the update program running you can type new information which will be added to the master file, and amendments and deletions. With the enquiry program running you can type requests for information which the computer will look up in the file, or work out from information in the file, and display as text on the screen. You can only use the report program if your computer has a printer, with which it can print information on paper. A report program prints documents based on the information in, or worked out from, the file, such as payslips if it's a payroll file (the term "report" is slightly misleading). Or it may print lists of information you select, such as a list of debtors if it's a customer file.

PACKAGES AND BESPOKE SOFTWARE

A business user may get a software house to write a program especially for him. This is called *bespoke* software. However it is extremely expensive and really outside the price range this book is about. A ready-written program is called *packaged software*, or simply a *package*. Some software houses are willing to tailor their packages, that is, write special versions for individual users, but this too is extremely expensive.

3.   Brief examples of uses

This section mentions some of the commonest types of programs as examples of what is available. Programs for business, home and other kinds of use are described. These are only descriptions of what is typical; one cannot say that a particular program you might buy would provide exactly the facilities described here. But chapter 4 will describe in detail several actual programs on the market.

PAYROLL

Maintains a file with a record for each person on your payroll. Each week, or whatever period you choose, you use the suite. You type each hourly-paid employee's hours worked, and other relevant information such as rates of pay, changes of salary for salaried employees, changes in tax rate etc. The suite updates the file, calculates pay and tax for each employee and prints out payslips and related documents.

STOCK CONTROL

Maintains a file showing what you have of each item you stock. Whenever you take something from stock you run the update program and type what you have taken and how much, and the program updates the file. Similarly when you buy extra stock. When you wish, you run the report programs, which print a list of current stock levels and a list of items you need to re-order. The suite may maintain a second file, in which you record the suppliers for each item, and may include a report program that will print the necessary orders.

WORD PROCESSOR

The word processor, well-known in many offices, is simply a computer with a word processor program built in. Such programs are available for many other micro-computers. You will probably want a more expensive printer than for other programs, so that the printing will look presentable if you use it for correspondence.

When running a word processor program a computer becomes a very superior typewriter. As you type a document, it is not immediately printed but is displayed on the screen. You can make corrections by typing over what is on the screen; the characters you type over simply disappear and are replaced by what you type now. Thus typing errors no longer mean using correction fluid or re-typing whole pages. You can even move text around, and insert or delete text. When you have finished you press a key and the computer prints the document. You can also make the computer record it in a file on disc so it can be displayed, altered or printed again whenever required. A word processor program may also automatically separate paragraphs, line up headings, produce a contents list and so on. It is especially useful if your work involves producing long documents such as manuals that need frequent revision.

MAILING LIST

Used, often together with a word processor, for generating circulars. You type a standard letter, but with blanks for information to be inserted which will be different on each copy. You have a file of people to be sent copies, and in each person's record are the words to be inserted in his copy of the circular. The program prints a copy of the circular for each person in the file, inserting the correct words in the blanks.

FINANCIAL PLANNING

Financial planning typically consists of estimating or deciding such things as production levels, sales, prices and expenditure over the next few months, and working out what cash flow and profits will be as a consequence. Often you want to try out different sets of figures and see how the results compare, to see what you should do in practice. Working out the results from each set of figures by hand can be very tedious.

With a financial planning program you describe to the program the calculation it's to do, and store in files the different sets of figures. The program will then display the cash flow forecast worked out from each set of figures. This takes only a few seconds, so you can quickly compare the alternatives and choose the best plan to follow.

BUDGET

With a budget program you can keep a file of your expenditure, with expenses under several headings such as (for a domestic use) food, insurance, travel and so on. Each evening, say, you type what you have spent in each category. Every month, or whatever period you choose, you can type what you estimate you will spend in the coming months. The program will display such things as your total expenditure in each category so far in the year, how much you have over- or under-spent this month compared to your previous estimates, a graph of your spending over the months, and so on.

BANK ACCOUNT

With a bank account program you keep track of how much you have in the bank. When you first use the program you type what your current balance is, and the program records this in a file. Each evening, say, you type details of cheques, standing orders and so on you have issued today, and of deposits, and the program updates its file in which it records your balance. It can really only be a rough guide. It can only be as accurate as you are careful to type details of your cheques and so on, and such things as bank charges, which may go out of your account without your even noticing, may change your real balance without your updating the computer's file.

TELEPHONE DIRECTORY

With a telephone directory program you keep a file with the names, addresses and telephone numbers of your acquaintances. To find out the telephone number of someone in the file you simply type their name, and the program displays their address and telephone number on the screen.

EDUCATION

An educational program contains, or comes with a data file that contains, a list of questions and answers on some subject such as maths or history. The program displays a question, and you type an answer. The program compares your answer to the answer it has, and displays a message saying whether you are right or wrong. It then displays another question.

Many programs for home computers are like this. They contain a fairly small number of questions, which they ask at random. Some are in effect simple quiz games. For more serious education a program may use the method that educationists have long called "programmed learning" (which here, unfortunately, is a confusing pun). The program displays explanations as well as questions, and the questions follow on from one another in a sensible order. It depends on whether you get a question right or wrong whether the program goes on to the next or displays a more detailed explanation of the part you got wrong and then further questions on it.

Unfortunately, serious educational software does not seem to be generally available.

BOARD AND CARD GAMES

Electronic games machines such as chess machines are in fact computers, with the program built in and with simplified and specialised screens and keyboards. Programs to play games like chess and bridge are available for many microcomputers. Some display a board on the screen, and display the pieces moving; others simply display messages telling you their moves.

With some programs you can set the level of skill you want the program to play at. This does not mean that if you set a low level the program makes deliberate mistakes. In a game like chess a computer really does take a long time to work out each move, and setting a level of skill limits the time the computer will spend, so it may well not find the best move.

VIDEO GAMES

Video game machines are in fact computers with the program built in and with simplified and specialised screens and keyboards. Programs for video games are available for many computers. The pictures that most computers can display are however not up to the standard of most arcade machines, and are often rather clumsy and stylised.

FANTASY GAMES

A fantasy game program displays on the screen pictures of, or messages describing, some imaginary realm such as a maze or labyrinth or a region of outer space. You have to imagine you are lost in this place, or have gone there with a mission such as finding treasure or defeating an alien fleet. Occasionally the program tells you of some danger approaching, such as a goblin or an alien spacecraft. You type messages saying what you will do, such as run away or fight. Generally the program decides at random the outcome of such decisions, consistent with what would be reasonable, and displays a message telling you.

All the time you are playing the program keeps count of your score, and keeps it displayed in a corner of the screen. Usually your score measures how long you've managed to stay alive so far, how much treasure you've acquired, or something such. Often there is no definite end to a game; you keep going until a monster eventually gets you, and the competition really is to see how your score compares with your score on previous occasions. Once you're experienced a game can last for hours.

Two very popular fantasy games are Adventure, in which you are in a labyrinth full of supernatural terrors, and Startrek, in which you are commanding the Starship Enterprise in search of Klingons or other aliens.

4.   What a computer consists of

The most obvious parts of a computer are the keyboard and the screen, which together are sometimes called the *console*.

Through these you control the computer and you enter and look up information. There is also a cassette tape recorder so the computer can record and playback (usually called *writing* and *reading*) tapes, or a similar but more advanced device called a *disc drive* for discs.

A disc drive may be a *floppy disc*, also called *diskette*, drive. You use this like a cassette recorder, having a library of floppy discs as you would of tape cassettes. Or it may be a *hard disc* drive. One hard disc has enough space on it for all the files you are likely to want to store, so a hard disc drive is often made with a disc fixed permanently on it; this is called a *Winchester* drive.

A computer using floppy discs usually has at least two floppy disc drives. Few computers have more than one tape recorder. Few people would need more than one hard disc drive, but often there is a floppy disc drive as well because programs for use on computers with hard discs are sold on floppy discs.

All these devices are connected to a *central processor* or *central processing unit (CPU)*. This does arithmetic and oversees the operation of the other devices. It constitutes the innards of the computer and the user hardly need be aware of it. Attached to the central processor is the *memory*. Despite its name this is a place where programs and data are stored **temporarily** while the CPU is working on them; the memory only works while the computer is turned on, and everything stored in it is erased when you switch off. The CPU can get instantly at anything in the memory, whereas data or programs on tape or disc it must copy into memory before it can do anything to them. If a program is too big to fit in your memory you cannot use it. You can usually buy additional chunks of memory.

The size of a file, or capacity of memory or any other data storage device, is measured in *bytes*. One byte is the space needed to hold one character. A larger unit is the *kilobyte* (abbreviated *Kb* or *K*), which is 1024 bytes. This is a convenient unit since for technical reasons memory is made in multiples of 1024 bytes. A larger unit again is the *megabyte* (abbreviated *Mb*), which is 1024 kilobytes.

A *microprocessor* or *microprocessing unit (MPU)* is a silicon chip forming an essential part of the central processor. A computer manufacturer buys microprocessors "off the shelf", and it is important to know what microprocessor your make of computer has. Some common ones are the *Zilog Z80*, the *Mostek 6502* and the *Intel 8080*.

All the devices connected to the CPU, apart from the memory, are called *peripherals*. Which ones are included in the basic machine varies. Often the basic machine consists of just a keyboard with the CPU and memory inside; you can buy a screen, properly called a *monitor*, and a cassette recorder, to plug in. With the great majority of computers you can use an ordinary television set, connected to the computer via the aerial socket, and a domestic tape recorder, connected via the socket most have for recording from or playing back through a radio.

Another peripheral, almost always an optional extra because it is expensive, is a *printer*. Most use *continuous, fanfold* stationery. This consists of a length of paper divided into sheets by perforations and fed vertically through the printer. More expensive printers use ordinary typing paper. The least expensive printers use narrow rolls of special, silver-coloured paper onto which they burn the characters.

There is an endless variety of other peripherals that you can buy for getting data in and out of a computer, besides the keyboard, screen and printer. However these others are more specialised and not so common. Some are described briefly in chapter 3.

Most peripherals are connected to the CPU via gadgets variously called *interfaces* or *controllers*. The user hardly need be aware of these; they are usually built into the peripheral or CPU.

You choose when buying a computer which peripherals to have. You can add more later, but be careful that the peripherals you want are available for your machine. As a general rule all the devices in your computer need to come from the same manufacturer's range, and for inexpensive machines some peripherals may not be made. CPU, memory, interfaces and controllers from different manufacturers won't work together because each manufacturer has his own *bus*, or internal wiring layout. However some manufacturers work to a standard, called *S100*. All properly designed S100 devices should work together, but here too there is a problem; there are several different versions of the standard.

Most computers simply plug into the mains. They actually need to be connected via a small device called a *power supply*, which adapts the power from the mains to the machine's needs, but this is normally built into the computer or its mains cable. But make sure you have enough sockets. You probably have a battery-powered cassette recorder, but the basic computer (that is, CPU and keyboard), television, disc drives and printer may all need to be plugged in separately.

5. Using the console

SCREEN FORMATS

The form in which data appears on the screen depends entirely on the program, but certain features are very common, and this section will describe them.

What you type usually appears as a line of text on the screen, each character appearing as you type it. This is to make typing easier, and is called *echo*. There is one character, called the *cursor*, always on the screen. It shows where the next character you type will appear, and it moves along as you type. It is usually a small flashing dash or block.

With most programs, the keyboard will only work when the program is ready for you to type. As soon as you start the program running it displays some message indicating it is ready and then waits for you to type. This message is called a *prompt*. If for example it's a file maintenance program, you now type which record you want to get at, and the data you want added to it (for an update) or a request for data (for an enquiry); or for a report a description of the report you want. The form in which you type these things is given in a manual for the program. You then press the key which on most computers is marked *send*, or *return*, or *newline*, and which takes the place of carriage-return on a typewriter. The program updates the record, or displays the requested information, and then displays the prompt again.

The commonest prompt is a single character, such as an asterisk, displayed at the bottom left of the screen with the cursor next to it. When after typing you press return (or *hit* return as people often say), everything on the screen moves up one line, or *scrolls up*. Thus each line you type remains visible until it disappears off the top of the screen.

Many computers can emit a short piercing bleep which a program can use to attract your attention. By analogy with a typewriter this is usually called the *bell*.

Also common is for the program to display a form on the screen. On the keyboard there are several keys called *cursor control keys*, with which you can move the cursor around. You fill in the blanks on the form using these keys to move from one blank to another. Like the details in a record, each space on a form is called a field.

A program that can perform several alternative tasks may display a *menu* on the screen. This is a list of the tasks the program can perform, with a number by each. You type the number of the task you want the program to do.

TYPING

The keyboard of a computer is very much like that of an electric typewriter, and typing is very much the same. There are a few differences, which this section will explain. The return and cursor control keys were explained in the last section.

It is not generally necessary to be a good typist to use a computer. When you are using a computer you are in effect conversing with it, and you spend as much time deciding what to type next as actually typing. However, if you have a lot of data to type, as when you are setting up a new file, then it may be useful. For this reason many business programs are designed with the expectation that you may give a secretary at least part of the job of running them.

Every computer has a button called something like *reset*, or *initialise*, or *break*. It is not really part of the keyboard, but is connected directly to the central processor. Pressing it makes the computer instantly stop whatever it is doing. After pressing reset it is as if you had just switched on, except that whatever was in the memory is still there.

There are times when the reset button must be used, but generally you should beware of it. Although it does not directly affect the files recorded on disc or tape, if you interrupt a program that is updating a file you cannot be sure in what state the file was left. On a few computers the reset button is badly placed, in that it can too easily be pressed accidentally.

Sometimes a computer keyboard has a key marked "control". It is rather like a second shift key. If you hold it down while pressing another key, say A, you get not lower case a or capital A, but a third version called *control-A*. It is not usually echoed, and there is no standard way of writing it (people sometimes write ↑ A) but a program can recognise it when you type it.

These characters are usually used for controlling a program. Many programs are written so that they stop, or take a particular action, when you type a particular character. Often such a program will take notice of one of these characters even when it has not prompted you to type.

Some computer keyboards have keys called *function keys*. These too are used for controlling programs; some programs are written so that they take a particular action when you press a particular function key.

The *rubout* or *backspace* key serves the same purpose as on a typewriter. It moves the cursor back so you can change what you have typed.

The digit zero and the letter "O" are not interchangeable on a computer. When writing something by hand in preparation for typing it into a computer people often cross their zeros thus Ø to avoid confusion. This convention of crossing zeros is widely used. It will be used in this book wherever it might otherwise not be clear that a zero is intended. It's also important to write the digit 1 and the letter "1" clearly so they will not be confused when typed.

It's usual to work entirely in capital letters on computers, except obviously when using such things as a word processor program. This is because many older computers do not have lower-case letters. This has given rise to the convention that when preparing something for typing into a computer people usually write in block capitals. People also write in block capitals when quoting something displayed or printed by a computer, which makes it unnecessary to use quotation marks. This convention too will be used in this book.

Characters other than letters and digits – punctuation marks, arithmetic signs and so on – are usually called *special characters*. A space – one press on the space bar – is often spoken of as a character like any other, and is often counted as a letter of the alphabet.

6. Controlling a computer

PROGRAMMING

Doing your own programming, whether for business, home or as a hobby, tends to be addictive and very time consuming. The set of instructions that a particular make of computer accepts is called its *machine code*. It depends on the microprocessor, and is described in a technical manual for the computer.

There is an easier way of programming than writing machine code. A *high-level language* is a standard language for writing programs. It too is a set of instructions you can use, but each instruction, called a *statement*, is a simple English-like phrase. For most computers there is a translation program available for each of the most popular high-level languages. You type your program into the computer and run the translation program, which translates it into the computer's machine code so it can be run.

People are occasionally confused by the idea of a translation program, thinking that such a program translates a program from one high-level language into another. In fact such programs are not unheard of (they are called *converters*) but they are extremely rare, as there is little call for them.

Chapters 5 onwards describe how you go about programming, and illustrate a variety of languages. There are many text-books available on the most popular high-level languages. By far the most popular for micro-computers is the language called *Basic*. Writing a simple program in Basic is no more difficult than using a calculator, but of course writing a complicated program is a long job in any language.

COMMANDS

You control a computer by typing simple phrases called *commands*. Each command makes it do some standard task such as copying one disc to another, running a progam etc. As soon as you switch on or hit reset the computer is ready to accept commands. It indicates that it is ready by displaying a prompt, and scrolls the screen up after each command.

A computer can carry out most commands, other than running a program, in a second or two; obviously how long a program takes depends on the program. Any lengthy single task, such as a program to be run, is called a *job*. The commands used on a particular make of computer are called its *command language* or *job control language (JCL)*. They are given in a manual for the computer.

Some programs, too, when running need you to type commands to tell them what to do. The commands for a particular program will be given in a manual for the program.

In short a command is something you type that the computer obeys straight away, as distinct from an instruction or statement, which is part of a program.

FILES ON TAPE AND DISC

Data is recorded on discs very compactly. A disc has room for many files; although a file may contain a lot of information it may occupy only a small area on a disc. Many commands are for handling files on disc. Examples are a command to make a copy of a file, and a command to erase, or *delete*, a file no longer wanted so the space can be re-used. Such commands take a computer only a few seconds to carry out, and are used frequently.

In a command to run a program that creates a new file you specify a name for the file, called its *filename*. The computer records this on the disc along with the file, and you can refer to the file by name in commands. When you run a program that needs to refer to the file you specify the name in the command, so that the program will read the correct file from the disc.

Usually the filename can be any string of letters and numbers you like, up to a certain length. Obviously you should not try to give two files on the same disc the same name. It is a good idea to give each file a name that shows what it is for.

On most computers, when a program needs to record a file on tape it displays a prompt asking you to set the tape recorder going. You position the tape where you want the file to begin, set it going, and hit return to make the program continue. Similarly with a program that reads a file you position the tape just before the start of the file and set it going. Many people prefer to keep only one file on each tape. Nevertheless on some computers files on tape have names just like files on disc.

PARAMETERS

A command usually consists of some fixed words, identifying the command, and some words you change each time you use the command. These latter are called *parameters*. For example, to make a copy of a file called ACCOUNTS (remember the convention of using capitals) and call the copy ACCOUNTS2, on many computers you would type

COPY ACCOUNTS TO ACCOUNTS2

The words ACCOUNTS and ACCOUNTS2 are the parameters.

Many programs require parameters, which you type as part of the command to run the program. What these parameters are, and what their effect is, is given in a manual for the program.

Other terms occasionally used to mean "parameter" are *option* and *argument*.

COMMAND FILES AND MACROS

Sometimes you find there is a particular sequence of commands you often want to use. On many computers you can store a sequence of commands in a file. Thereafter you can simply type the name of the file and the computer will carry out the commands in it. In effect you have added a new command to the computer's repertoire, to do what previously you had to type several commands to do. This file is called a *command file*.

There are several other terms in common use to mean "command file". Some common ones are *steering file* and *submit file*.

This new command may itself have parameters. If it does it is called a *macro*.

LOADING PROGRAMS

A program must be *loaded*, that is, read from its program file into memory, each time it is run; it is the copy in memory that runs. Every computer has a command to load a program, and often one command both loads it and runs it. On some computers this command consists simply of typing the name of the program file containing the program, followed by any parameters the program requires.

When you load a program it replaces, or *overwrites*, whatever is in the part of memory where it is put. The memory may be big enough for several programs, but very few micro-computers are capable of being *multi-programmed*, or interspersing the execution of one program with the execution of another so they effectively run simultaneously, as is done on big computers.

OPENING AND CLOSING FILES

When a program creates a new file, before it writes the first record it records some technical information about it on the disc or tape. This is called *opening* the file. When a program reads a file it must start off by reading this information; this too is called opening the file. Some more such information is written or read when a program has finished writing or reading a file, and this is called *closing* the file.

As a user you don't really need to know this, but the terms are explained here because they are often heard.

7. Types of update

To process a record, either to update it or to get information from it, a program must read it, that is, copy it into memory. If a program updates a file by reading each record, amending it in memory, and then writing it back to the same place, it does an *update-in-place*. It may instead make a new copy of the whole file; it reads the file into memory, amends there the records that are to be amended, then writes this new version on to the tape or a new place on the disc. This is called a *batch update*.

If a program does an update-in-place you might well run it whenever there is new data to be added to the file. With the more cumbersome batch update you would probably save new data up for a periodical run.

8. Tape, floppy disc and hard disc

The most important feature of any computer is whether you keep your files on tape, floppy disc or hard disc.

Data is recorded on a disc the same way as on a tape cassette; each character is represented by a magnetic pattern. A floppy disc is a disc some inches across made of the same stuff as recording tape. You insert the disc in a slot in the drive, where it sits on a revolving turntable. The record/playback head, usually called a *read/write head*, is mounted on an arm which can move across the disc. Data is recorded on the disc in circular tracks.

The head moves very fast, and a program can control its movements precisely, so a program can get at any record on a disc very quickly. In contrast a tape once started moves along at a constant, and relatively slow, speed, and a program looking for a particular record must simply wait until it is reached. This makes using tape very restrictive.

Firstly, loading a program from tape takes minutes, compared to seconds with disc. Secondly, a program can't search around the tape for a particular record, so to do any update or answer any enquiry it must first load the whole file into memory. This again may take many minutes, and it means the data file and the program processing it mustn't together be bigger than your memory. With a file on disc even a program doing a batch update can avoid this limitation by reading and writing the file a bit at a time.

A hard disc works in the same way as a floppy disc, but it has a much larger capacity, is rigid and often fixed to the drive. This avoids a couple of irritations of floppy discs. Firstly, although putting the right floppy discs for a program in the drives (called *loading* the discs) takes only a few seconds, it can be annoying if you run many short jobs. Secondly, a floppy disc soon fills up, compelling you to spend some minutes either deleting old versions of files (left behind after batch updates) or copying files to a new disc. With a hard disc you should occasionally delete old copies to make room, but generally you will have more than enough space for your files.

A floppy disc drive costs much more than a cassette tape recorder, and a hard disc drive costs much more again. Chapter 3 includes a rough guide to prices.

3
BUYING AND USING
A COMPUTER

1. Some common terms

As in chapter 2 we will start off by introducing and
commenting on some terms in common use.

Input and *output*	"Input" is information that you enter into a computer, or that is read from a peripheral into memory. "Output" is information obtained from a computer, or written from memory to a peripheral. People also talk of "inputting" and "outputting" information; to "put information in" a program would mean to include it as part of the program.
To *move*	To "move" data or a program almost always means to copy it; it does not imply that the original is deleted. It is important to remember this, because this term is often used.
Printout, report, listing, document, to *print out*	When a computer prints something on paper it is often said to "print it out", and the resulting printed paper is called a printout, report, listing or document.
To *store*	To "store" data or a program means to move (copy) it to a place of more permanent storage; thus from memory to disc or tape.
System	An overworked term. Can mean a computer and all its programs, or some set of programs, or, especially, an operating system (see this chapter).

31

To *type in, key in*   When you type something at a computer
you are often said to "type it in" or
"key it in".

2.   Common system software

Programs that make a computer do useful tasks are called
application(s) programs. There are also programs that make
the computer easier to use, and these are called *system(s)
programs*. Even if you do your own programming you would
not attempt to write system programs; they are extremely
complex and writing them is a very specialised job. They are
best regarded like devices, as parts of the computer system to
be bought.

Some system programs are essential. The most necessary
are not sold on disc or tape, but are built into the computer by
being recorded indelibly, when the machine is made, in a
special part of memory called the *read-only-memory* (*ROM*).
Far from being erased, as the contents of the rest of memory
are, when the computer is switched off, the contents of ROM
can never be erased or altered. The programs in ROM are
called the computer's *firmware*.

Some system programs are needed only by people writing
their own applications programs. This section describes the
system programs that you are likely to need whether or not
you do your own programming. A later section describes the
ones you are likely to need if you do program.

MONITOR

A computer without a program running will do nothing
whatever; a computer obeys commands because of a program
called a *monitor* (see also "monitor", page 22). This is in the
ROM, and starts running as soon as you switch on or hit reset.
This is often called *bootstrapping*, or *booting*, from the
expression "pick yourself up by the bootstraps". The monitor
runs continually, awaiting or obeying commands, except when
some other program is running. When a program finishes and
the monitor starts up again we say the program *returns to* or
returns control to the monitor.

A running program can *call* the monitor, that is, activate it
temporarily to do some task. When the task is done the

monitor returns to the program, which then continues. A programmer knows the facilities offered by the monitor of the computer he is writing for, and writes his program to use them. Thus a program might not work if the monitor were changed. Manufacturers seldom do change their monitors, except to add facilities.

The facilities offered by a monitor are quite primitive, and are insufficient for the needs of many programs. In particular a monitor is unlikely to offer convenient facilities for using disc drives. For more advanced facilities see the next section.

OPERATING SYSTEMS

An *operating system* is a program that works like a monitor, but offers much more comprehensive facilities. Most important are the facilities a program needs to use discs easily. An operating system is often not built in, but is bought on tape or disc, and your first act after switching on or hitting reset is to type a monitor command to load it. Some computers will load it automatically if there is a disc containing it on a drive when you switch on or hit reset.

In fact it is more accurate to describe an operating system as a set of programs, because in addition to the main one there are usually several separate ones that automatically come into action to carry out particular commands that you type.

Each manufacturer produces his own operating system, but there is a standard one called *CP/M* available for most computers with Z80 or 8080 microprocessors. Most commercially available programs require your computer to have the appropriate operating system, rather than just the monitor.

"BASIC" INTERPRETER

As well as home-written programs, many programs are sold in the Basic language. The translation program you need to run a Basic program is called an *interpreter*. It works rather like a monitor. Once running it waits for commands. You type a command for it to load a program, or you load a new home-written program by typing it into the computer (you can then type a command to store it on tape or disc). You then type a command to run the program, and the interpreter goes through it one statement at a time, translating and executing each statement in turn. When the program finishes ("returns to Basic") you can type commands to load and run another program, or to return to the monitor or operating system.

If you wish you can type a command to *list* the program that is in memory, that is, display the text of the program on the screen. You can alter the program in memory by altering what's on the screen.

With the interpreter running you can also use a Basic statement like a command, simply typing it for the computer to obey straight away. Since many statements are instructions to work out calculations, this means you can use the computer like a calculator. It also means that if you are unfamiliar with the language you can easily experiment to see what a statement does, if it is not clear from your manual or text-book on Basic.

There are Basic interpreters available for virtually all computers. Some computers in fact have a Basic interpreter in ROM, in place of a monitor. This makes using the computer very simple, but means that only programs in Basic can be run.

Although Basic is supposed to be standardised, in fact the computer manufacturers and software houses that write interpreters and Basic programs work to many slightly different versions of it. These different versions are called *dialects*. Because of this you can never assume that a program written in Basic for one make of computer will work on another without a programmer amending it. This is true of all high-level languages (still it is an improvement on machine code, which is completely different for each make of microprocessor).

Basic is the only widely used language translated by interpreters. Most high-level languages use another kind of translation program, described later in this chapter. There are in fact some dialects of Basic that use this other kind of translation program too.

3. Errors

Needless to say a computer cannot tell if what you type is incorrect; but it can tell if what you type is impossible. If, for example, you type a command to delete a non-existent file, or you give somebody's hours worked as "J. Smith", a properly written program will display an *error message* pointing out your mistake; you can then type what you really meant. These checks that a program makes are called *validation* or *vetting*. The error messages usually describe nonsensical data as "invalid" or "illegal".

A mistake that prevents the program running at all – such as forgetting to put the disc containing a needed data file onto a drive – is called a *fatal error* or *terminal error*. The program should display an error message telling you what's wrong, and finish, returning to the monitor or operating system. You then correct the mistake and run the program again.

However, programs are not always so perfect. A badly written program may accept nonsensical data and put it in the file. Worse still, it may be unable to continue. It may either display a fatal error message and finish (irritating if your mistake was a minor one) or *crash*, which means the computer simply stops and the keyboard will not work – you have to hit reset before you can use the computer again. A program that goes wrong like this while updating a file is a considerable nuisance, as you do not know how much of the updating it did.

If, after you have typed something and the computer has accepted it, you realise that it was incorrect, you will want to change it. With a well designed program you can easily do so, but with a badly designed program it may be quite difficult.

An error in a program is called a *bug*. While a bug that affected the handling of correct data would obviously be intolerable, a few software houses seem to regard bugs and shortcomings like those described above as merely unfortunate.

Some programs, though, especially some system programs, are so extremely complicated that they may contain subtle, rarely noticed bugs however conscientious the software house. For such a program the software house should take care to notify users of any bugs discovered, and perhaps to issue corrected copies of the program.

There are many colloquial expressions to do with errors. A program is said to *come up with*, or *flag*, an error message. Words for "crash" include *blow up, bomb out, fall over, fall apart*, and many others.

4. Back-up

The one disadvantage of being able to keep and process files so easily is that you can accidentally destroy them easily too. Absent-mindedly typing the wrong filename in a "delete file" command, or spilling coffee on a disc, can destroy an awful lot of data; and no matter how careful you are it will happen from time to time.

The solution is simple. Keep a copy (called a *back-up* copy or *security* copy) of every disc or cassette, and every time you update a disc or cassette copy it anew. Most computers have a command to copy one floppy disc to another, provided you have two drives. If you have only one drive or have only a tape recorder this may not be possible, because then to copy a disc or cassette the computer must read the entire contents into memory and then write them all out again after you put on a new one; the memory may not be big enough.

Backing up hard discs is a problem, since you probably only have one drive, with a disc fixed in place. Various devices are available, such as a tape recorder built into the drive purely for taking back-ups. Some drives have two turntables, one with a fixed disc and one for removeable discs; with these you can use removeable discs for back-up copies.

You can back-up an individual file that is on disc simply by making a copy of the file. Any computer should have a command to copy a file on disc. If the copy is on the same disc the file is of course not protected against accidents that damage the disc, but at least it is protected against being accidentally deleted. There is a convenient way to back up a file maintained by batch updates. After running the update program, don't delete the old generation of the file. Keep it, and keep the data (presumably written on paper) that was used for the update, until after the next time you run the update program. Thus if you lose the latest generation of the file you can re-create it by re-doing the update run that created it.

Be careful when taking back-ups. Ironically it is one of the most dangerous times for a file; you only have to get the parameters the wrong way round in a copy command and you may find you have copied some other file into the file you meant to make a copy of. When you copy a file into a file that already exists, the data is generally not added on the end; it completely overwrites what is already there.

5.   File organisation

The *organisation* of a file is the way the records are laid out within it. It is the affair of the programmer writing the programs to maintain the file, but as advertisements for programs often mention the organisation that a program will use for the master file it will create and maintain, even people not intending to write their own programs should at least be familiar with the terms.

The great majority of files have one field that appears in every record and that identifies the record. It is the personnel number in a personnel file, the account number in an accounts file, and so on. It is called the *key field*, and the number in a particular record's key field is called that record's *key*. When you are using a file maintenance program you usually indicate what record you want to get at by typing its key.

To *access* a record or a file means to read it or write to it. If a program starts at the beginning of a file and accesses every record in turn it is said to access the file *sequentially*. If it just accesses individual records it is said to access them *directly*. For direct access the program must know from the key just where the record must be; in theory it could read through the file till it came to the required record but in practice this takes too long.

There are three common types of file organisation, called *sequential*, *relative* and *indexed sequential*.

In a sequential file the records are stored one after another in order of key. A program cannot tell from the key exactly where on the disc or tape each record will be, so a sequential file can only be accessed sequentially. It can only be updated by batch update, not by update-in-place. On tape this is the only kind of organisation possible.

In a relative file there is a fixed place on the disc for each record. The records are stored in order of key, but if any key is unused – for example if record 3 is followed by record 5 – the space for the missing record is left empty. Records can only be accessed directly; the file cannot be accessed sequentially as the program would try to read the missing records. The file is updated by update-in-place.

In an indexed sequential file the records can be in any order. There is a second file, called the *index*, with a record, or entry, for each record in the main file. Each entry has two fields, giving the key and *address*, or position on the disc, of the corresponding main record; the field containing the address is called a *pointer*. The index itself is sequential, and because it is small, with only two fields in each record, a program can read the whole index into memory preparatory to processing the file.

An indexed sequential file can be accessed sequentially or its records accessed directly. In either case the program reads the copy of the index in memory sequentially. In the first case it processes the record indicated by each successive index entry, and in the second case it reads through the index till it reaches the entry for the required record. Because the index is in memory this can be done extremely quickly. An indexed sequential file is updated by update-in-place, the index itself being updated in memory and then written back to its old place.

6. Kits

Many computers, even those intended for small businesses, can be bought as kits. This is a legacy of the very early days of micro-computers when they were aimed mainly at hobbyists. Needless to say, only people with some interest in electronics should buy kits! Other people may prefer to skip this section, which merely describes enough of the insides of a computer to introduce the commonest terms.

The purely electronic parts of a computer – the CPU, memory, interfaces and controllers – each occupy a separate *printed circuit board (PCB)*, also called a *card* or simply a *board*. This is a board, usually about 10″ by 8″, with the electronic components soldered onto it, connected to one another by copper *tracks* printed on the board. *Signals*, currents with specific meanings, travel along the tracks from one component to another. Each track is for a particular signal. Each interface or controller has a cable going to the appropriate peripheral.

The major part of making a kit is soldering the components in place on the boards. Many of these components are silicon chips, more properly called *integrated circuits (ICs)*. A silicon chip is a small wafer of silicon, enclosed in protective plastic, with an electronic circuit etched in it. They are mass-produced for use in machines such as computers. The other components are referred to as *discrete* components.

Each board must be able to send signals to the other boards, and to receive signals from them. For this purpose most of the tracks finish at one edge of the board. This row of tracks is the bus mentioned in chapter 2 (from the Latin "omnibus", meaning "for all", since it carries all the signals between boards). The end of each track, at the edge of the board, is called a *contact*. The boards are all plugged into an extra board called a *motherboard*, which has on it simply a row of long narrow sockets; the edge of each board with the contacts is pushed into a socket. The sockets are connected together by tracks on the motherboard, thus joining up the busses of all the boards. Sometimes there is no separate motherboard; instead the CPU board has several slots on it for other boards to be plugged into.

All this assumes that the busses of all the boards have the same layout, with the track for each signal in the same position in all of them. In general each manufacturer has his own bus layout, so all your boards have to come from the same manufacturer. However, as chapter 2 mentioned, some manufacturers make boards to a common standard, enabling the buyer to use together boards from any of them. A computer made up in this way is called a *homebrew* computer. Unfortunately there are several rival standards. The most widely followed is the S100 standard, so called because the bus has 100 tracks, but there are several slightly different versions even of this. Other standards are *SS50* and *Eurocard*.

A motherboard or CPU board with several boards plugged into it at right angles is obviously prone to knocks. The whole is therefore often mounted in a frame called a *card cage* or *mainframe* (this word is also used to mean a big, multi-million pound computer). The motherboard or CPU board is screwed into the card cage; the other boards, when they are plugged into the sockets, are held in place by slots in the card cage called *card guides*.

Also in the computer is a power supply. This is an electric circuit from which comes the cable to plug into the mains; in fact it may be built into this cable. It takes the power coming from the mains and produces the much lower voltages the computer needs. It is connected by wires to the tracks in the bus that carry the power to the different boards.

7. Power of a computer

The most important measure of the power of a computer is the size of its memory. This is because it must load an entire program into memory in order to execute it (admittedly a programmer may *segment* his program, that is, write it in sections that are loaded in turn, but this repeated loading makes it very slow to run). Most small business computers come with at least 16 kilobytes. Home computers may come with as little as 1Kb, which is fine for learning about computers and for simple programs, though you will soon want to buy additional memory to expand it to around 16Kb. Most computers can be expanded up to 64Kb.

Also very important is the kind of file storage device used. Replacing a cassette recorder with a pair of floppy drives, or replacing these with a hard disc drive, adds to speed, convenience and the kinds of program that can be run so greatly that it's like using a different machine. The differences were described in chapter 2.

The speed at which the central processor executes instructions is also a measure of a computer's power. Since a typical CPU executes about half-a-million instructions per second this may not seem to make much practical difference. But some system programs are very complicated; for example an interpreter executing a Basic program must translate each statement into machine code, a complex task, and as it does so parts of the interpreter may be executed over and over many times. So the speed of the CPU can make an appreciable difference.

The unit of speed for a CPU is the *megahertz* (abbreviated *Mhz*), which is one million cycles per second; the cycle refers to an internal rhythm of the CPU, and a typical instruction takes several cycles. Most CPUs operate at 2 or 4Mhz.

8. Buying a computer

This section lists some points that should be remembered in buying a computer.

1) Small firms sometimes make the mistake that big companies used to; they buy a computer in the belief that it will be generally useful, then ask what programs are available for it. If you do this in buying a computer for business you may have to change the whole way you run your business just to suit the available programs! The right approach is to decide what tasks you want a computer to do and buy one for which the necessary programs are available. It's the software that you have to live with – all you require of the hardware is that it includes the devices necessary to run the software and store all your files, and that it doesn't break down too often.

2) Even if you plan to do your own programming you'll almost certainly want to buy programs as well, especially at first when you would otherwise be using the computer for nothing other than learning to program.

3) If you are thinking of buying an expensive machine, and feel you would like some practical experience of computers first, consider buying an inexpensive computer as a prelude. Some cost no more (and are no bigger) than a good calculator, and can be bought over-the-counter as easily. Although their storage capacity may be limited, and they are designed for convenience rather than flexibility, they are good machines, and to use are enough like other computers to enable you to see in practice much of what this book explains.

4) Computers, like all machines, break down. Find out what after-sales service is available for your machine.

5) As chapter 1 said, buying a computer is like buying a hi-fi system; you choose devices separately, though usually from the same range. While a computer costing £300 will do some useful tasks, the extra devices to turn it into a powerful business machine may double or quadruple the price. Page 45 gives a rough guide to prices.

6) Computers are among the few things in the world whose prices are constantly dropping. This is because the technology is constantly advancing and the market expanding, and from time to time drops in prices are spectacular. At the time of writing (1982), most computers

intended for home use cost around £200 to £300, although there are now some good ones for much less than £100. Disc drives cost about £200, which puts them beyond the reach of most home users, but undoubtedly much cheaper ones are about to appear. For many people this may make a home computer for the first time a worthwhile proposition. Take for example an enquiry program such as the telephone directory program mentioned in chapter 1; as long as it has to be loaded from tape it might seem more convenient simply to keep a list on paper, but a disc is much quicker and more convenient.

7) There will be more software on the market for a popular make of computer than for a less popular make.

8) Computers differ considerably in detail, and even an experienced user needs a clear instruction manual. Some computers have very poor manuals; take this into account when choosing.

9) A chapter intended to "fill you in" on the lore of micro-computers would be incomplete if it didn't tell you the names of some well-known ones, so here are a few; the Apple III, Superbrain, Exidy Sorcerer, Apple II, Commodore Pet, Tandy TRS-80, BBC Microcomputer, Commodore Vic-10, -20, and -30, Sinclair Spectrum, Acorn Atom, Sinclair ZX81. But it must be emphasized that these are only a few of the many good and popular machines.

The above list is roughly in order of price, with expensive business machines first and inexpensive home machines last. But again in some cases cheapness is a sign of modern design, not of lack of power.

The BBC Microcomputer is designed and built by the Acorn company, and partly intended to accompany a BBC educational series on computers.

10) When buying a machine remember that you may well want to buy additional devices later, and that – especially in business – your needs may change as time goes by. Make sure any additional devices you may want are available for the machine.

11) You should think of having many programs for your computer and using it for many different things. To use a machine designed for versatility for only one or two tasks may be a great waste.

9. Buying programs

This section lists some points that should be remembered in buying programs.

1) What information you keep in a file, what calculations the computer will do on that file, and in what form you get information in and out depends on the program or suite maintaining that file. When you buy a business program or suite you are buying the facility to keep a particular file.

2) Programs are advertised either for a particular computer, or for say "any Z80 computer running under CP/M", in other words any computer with a Z80 microprocessor and equipped with the operating system CP/M. A program will only run on the machines it's written for. You must also make sure your computer has all the devices that the program needs, enough memory for the program to fit in, and any systems programs (such as an interpreter) the program needs.

3) When buying a program to do some important part of your business, ask yourself not only if it does what you want now, but if you may want to change your method of working in the future, and if the program might make such changes difficult.

4) A program should be *user-friendly*, that is, the messages it displays and forms of input it expects should be in reasonably plain English.

5) What a program does if you type nonsense is important, for everyone makes typing mistakes. It should give an error message, not accept the nonsense without comment or crash. Also, if you enter data that is sensible but incorrect, a program should let you correct it.

6) To know how to use a program you need an instruction manual with it. These are sometimes poorly written and produced; take this into account when choosing.

7) The software industry has the same problem as the music industry; just as with the taping of gramophone records, people sometimes copy programs that friends have bought rather than buying them themselves. This makes the industry less profitable than it might otherwise be, and so means fewer programs are put on the market.

Firms selling expensive business programs usually try to overcome this by keeping a register of purchasers, and having a standard contract that licences the buyer to use the program only on his own computer, and to take copies only for back-up. It usually goes together with after-sales support; they agree to send you a corrected version if a bug is found or if data built into the progam changes, to give you advice and so on. Someone using an illegitimate copy would, lacking these things, probably find such a program difficult to use.

Firms selling inexpensive software, whether for business or home, by mail order or through a high street retailer, obviously cannot do this. They tend to rely on their software being cheap enough for copying not to be worthwhile.

8) A large business suite will come on a floppy disc, maybe several if one is too small for all the programs. If your computer has a hard disc you copy the contents of the floppies onto it. If your computer uses floppy discs you take enough blank floppies to contain the programs, you copy the operating system (which you have bought previously, probably with the computer) onto each, and then you copy the new programs onto these discs. In either case you store the original discs, called master discs or issue discs, away as back-ups.

9) Sometimes a business package needs an *initialisation run*. This means it must be run once, before you start to use it, for some special jobs to be done. Often the dealer will do this run for you. For example a package may be unable to work without a master file already existing; the initialisation run will create a master file, though with no records in it. Another thing commonly needed is *configuring*; typing such information as the kind of VDU you have, the width of paper your printer uses, and so on. Also your company name may be put into the program, so it can be printed at the top of your reports (this also discourages illicit copying of programs).

10) The main work for you is when you first get the program. Someone has to type into the computer all the information that is to be kept on file. Thereafter you will only need to make changes as they come. This typing is work that your secretary or a clerk might do.

10.   Points to remember

This section lists some points that should be borne in mind to avoid common errors and misconceptions.

1) You can't possibly damage the hardware by what you type.

2) Do not expect to turn the computer on and off each time you use it. Many computers are intended to be left on all day.

3) Messages a computer displays are not messages from the computer any more than messages written on paper are messages from the paper. They are messages from the person who wrote the program.

4) Don't blame the computer. At least, not the hardware. If your computer produces a bill for 5 million jelly babies for Mrs. Jones it's probably because you typed that she bought 5 million jelly babies. Just occasionally it may be because of a bug. Actual hardware faults causing such mistakes are extremely rare (hence the infamous saying "computers don't make mistakes").

5) An excuse firms sometimes use is "now your order's in the computer we can't get at it". This is strange, because the purpose of keeping information on a computer is to enable you to get at it easily. Nevertheless, it may be true; a program may not produce the output needed to answer the customer's query, or may provide no way of correcting incorrect data on file. The firm should choose or write its programs more carefully.

6) If you use your computer to produce sensitive items, such as final demands, check them before posting – don't leave the ultimate responsibility for such things to a piece of office equipment.

11.   Details of hardware

This section describes separately the devices introduced in chapter 2, with additional details. Notes on capacity and price are included, but it must be emphasised that inevitably these are just very rough estimates of what is average at the time of writing. There is a tremendous range, and you get what you pay for, though prices tend to drop – sometimes spectacularly – with each new product.

Later sections briefly introduce some less common peripherals that may be of interest to some readers.

CENTRAL PROCESSOR

When you've chosen your computer you've chosen your CPU. Probably about £100 of a computer's price is the CPU, and of this about £10 is the microprocessor. This £10, perhaps more than the microprocessor's small size, constitutes the "miracle of the chip"; a few years ago equivalent equipment cost more like £100,000.

Most present-day microprocessors are *8-bit*. There is no need to explain this technical term; suffice it to say that eventually they will probably be superseded by the more powerful *16-bit* microprocessors.

One specific point is worth mentioning; the Zilog Z80 was developed from the Intel 8080, and accepts all the instructions an 8080 does and more. This means programs for the Z80 generally run faster and are – for someone programming in machine code – easier to write, but also means any program written for the 8080 will work on a Z80.

MEMORY

The memory consists of two types of memory, the ROM described in section 2 and the *RAM (random access memory,* an utterly meaningless term but we're stuck with it), which is the central processor's work area as described in chapter 2. For some computers you can buy extra ROM containing extra parts of the monitor, or Basic interpreter if one is built in instead, to gave extra facilities. A computer comes with a certain amount of RAM, perhaps 1K on a hobby machine, perhaps 16K on the smallest business machine, and you can buy more. On most present-day micro-computers the total ROM and RAM cannot exceed 64K, although on some recent machines the limit is much higher. RAM costs about £50 for 8K, but for some machines is much cheaper.

RAM is either *static* or *dynamic*. The difference is in the principles they work on. Both function in the same way, and to the user the only difference is that static RAM is slightly more reliable and slightly more expensive.

KEYBOARD

The keyboard is invariably built in. It accounts for about £40 of the price. Some cheaper computers have *touch-sensitive keyboards*; these are like ordinary keyboards, but each key is just a touch-sensitive patch. These are cheaper, around £20, but a little difficult to get used to. Some keyboards, in addition to all the usual keys, have a *numeric key-pad*, a separate group of keys for the digits 0-9.

SCREEN

Usually called a *visual display unit (VDU)* or *video*. Strictly speaking these terms refer to the interface (worth about £100) connecting the screen to the CPU, and the screen itself is called a monitor or a *CRT (for cathode ray tube)*. A monitor, if none is built in, costs about £100 for a black-and-white one, but on most computers you can use a television set. There is a cable from the interface which you plug into the aerial socket. The interface needs to be connected to a TV via a small device called an *RF modulator*, but probably has one built in – it adds only a few pounds to the cost.

One important characteristic of a VDU is whether it displays in colour or black and white. To get colour both your monitor (or TV) and the VDU proper (the interface) must be colour. A second important characteristic is whether in addition to everyday characters it can display *graphics* characters, assorted shapes from which a program can make pictures, graphs etc. This depends on the VDU proper but not on the monitor.

CASSETTE TAPE RECORDER

If one isn't built in you can use any tape recorder, provided your computer incorporates a *cassette interface*. (Despite this emphasis on the more modern cassette recorder, a reel-to-reel recorder could equally well be used for storing data and programs you write yourself; but programs you buy will come on cassettes.) Most computers have a cassette interface built in; it adds only a few pounds to the cost. The only advantage of a tape recorder over a disc drive is its price of around £40. Chapter 2 compared the usefulness of tape and disc.

It is best, if using a domestic tape recorder, to have one where the loudspeaker can be turned off so it does not play back out loud when plugged into the computer. Otherwise you will hear the program, a shrill bleeping, whenever you load – and the computer (receiving the program along the wire) usually needs the volume turned up loud.

You can use ordinary tape cassettes. But it is better to use cassettes made specially for use with computers, called *digital cassettes*.

FLOPPY DISC DRIVE

Described in section 8 of chapter 2. Most floppy disc drives take standard discs 8″ in diameter, but some slightly cheaper ones take 5¼″ *mini-floppies*. Many drives are *double-density*, which means they squeeze twice as much data onto a disc as older designs of drive did.

A floppy disc drive costs about £200, though this may soon fall. For business use you will probably want two, not only for backing discs up but because it is often convenient to have the operating system and program files on one and data files on the other. You also need a floppy disc controller, costing about £100. One controller can handle several drives, and it may be built into a drive.

A floppy disc costs a few pounds, and they are usually sold in packs of about ten. An 8″ disc recorded in double-density has a capacity of about 400K or about half a million characters.

A floppy disc is enclosed in a square cardboard cover for protection. You do not take this off; there are slots in it through which the read/write head and the hub of the turntable can touch the disc. The disc and cover together come in a cardboard cover which you do take off.

HARD DISC DRIVE

Described in section 8 of chapter 2. The typical capacity of a Winchester drive is about 10Mb and a typical price is about £1000. Hard disc drives with removable (usually called *exchangeable*) discs are common on more expensive computers.

PRINTER

A printer works very slowly compared with the rest of a computer, and whereas a screenful of text can be displayed in a few seconds the same text can take more than a minute to print. A long report can therefore be the most time-consuming part of a job.

The commonest size of continuous stationery has space for 120 characters on a line and about 60 lines per page. The printer can be adjusted to the width you use. *Special stationery* such as sheets of sticky labels, or pre-printed forms for common applications, is available as continuous stationery.

There are several standards for the way a printer is wired up. Provided your printer and printer interface are made to the same standard they will work together even if they come from different manufacturers. The commonest standard is called RS232.

Many printers are *dot matrix* printers. This means that each character is composed of tiny dots. The resulting print quality, though not as good as a typewriter, is adequate for most purposes.

A printer as described costs around £400. However for some purposes you may want a *correspondence quality*, or *letter quality*, printer, which prints on ordinary typing paper and with a quality as good as an electric typewriter. Such a printer costs about £1000.

A very cheap kind of printer is the *electrostatic printer*, which prints on a narrow roll of special, silver-coloured paper onto which it burns the characters. These generally cost less than £100.

Some less common peripherals which are of specialised interest

SOUND EFFECTS

Many computers for home use have peripherals, usually built in, through which a program can produce sound effects. These are intended for use with video games. Sometimes programs can play tunes through these, but on many the notes are little more than bleeps.

JOYSTICK

A *joystick* is used mainly for games. It is a small lever like those on video games machines, and is used for the same purpose, controlling the movement of shapes on the screen.

MODEM

A *modem* is a device for connecting a computer to a telephone line so it can send data (or programs) to, or receive it from, distant computers. You have to get British Telecom's approval to connect it to your telephone.

A cheaper alternative is an *acoustic modem*; you clip the telephone receiver onto this and the modem bleeps into the mouthpiece and picks up the bleeps from the distant computer's modem from the earpiece. Since this is not wired into the telephone it does not need approval.

ANALOGUE-TO-DIGITAL CONVERTER

An *analogue-to-digital converter (ADC)* is a device for connecting a computer to some electrical instrument or machinery so the computer can monitor it. The ADC constantly measures the voltage in any electrical circuit it is connected into and sends the measurements to the CPU. A program would be constantly running to accept the measurements.

DIGITAL-TO-ANALOGUE CONVERTER

A *digital-to-analogue converter (DAC)* is a device for connecting a computer to some electrical machinery so the computer can control it. The DAC controls the voltage in any electrical circuit it is connected into in accordance with data the CPU constantly sends it. A program would be constantly running to produce the data.

VOICE INPUT UNIT

A *voice input unit* is a peripheral that you speak to. Present models mis-hear words quite often, so for most people this is still something for the future.

VOICE OUTPUT UNIT

A *voice output unit*, or *speech synthesiser*, is a peripheral that speaks. Present models have a limited vocabulary, so for most people this is still something for the future.

12. System software

Section 2 on page 32 described the system programs that most users would want. But many system programs are needed only by people writing their own applications programs, and these are described here. Other readers may like to get to know the names for these programs as these names will often be heard.

COMPILER

A *compiler*, like an interpreter, enables a computer to carry out a program written in a high-level language, but its approach is different. It translates the entire program into machine code and stores the translated program (the *object program*) in a new file. It is said to *generate* the object program. Now you can load and execute this object program just as if it had been written in machine code in the first place. The original program (the *source program*) is also kept, for reference.

The advantage of a compiler over an interpreter is that executing an object program is much faster than interpreting a source program. Also some high-level languages, like Basic, are for technical reasons more suitable for interpreting while others are more suitable for compiling. The best known of these latter are:

Cobol – the traditional language for business programs on big computers, and also widely available on the larger micro-computers.

Pascal – becoming popular for micro-computers; sometimes suggested as replacing Basic in the future, though it is less suitable for beginners.

There are also some dialects of Basic for which you can buy either compilers or interpreters.

Some compilers produce the object program in a code, often called *intermediate code* or *pseudo-code (p-code)* that is not the computer's machine code. The object program then has to be interpreted. This enables the software house to sell the same compiler, itself in the intermediate code, for different makes of computer, with just a different interpreter for each make. Such an interpreter is a comparatively simple program since the compiler does most of the work. Thus the user still gets the advantage of reasonably fast execution.

EDITOR

If you use an interpreter to run a program you have written, you simply type the program while the interpreter is running, and when you have finished you type a command to store it or run it. With a compiler however you must put the program into a file before running the compiler.

An *editor* enables you to type a new file onto the computer or make alterations to an existing one. Since data files are set up and maintained by programs, an editor is normally only needed for program files. There are two types of editor. A *screen editor* works like a word processor; it displays the file on the screen, one screenful at a time, and you add to or alter what's on the screen. With a *line editor* you type commands to make the editor find strings of characters which you specify in the command, and to alter them, delete them or insert new characters before them. Some editors provide both kinds of facilities.

Generally editors do batch updates.

LINKAGE EDITOR

On a large micro-computer you may have a program called a *linkage editor*. It is sometimes convenient to write a large program in several parts, called modules, and compile or assemble them one at a time as if they were separate programs. The object modules produced then have to be joined together. A linkage editor, or *link editor*, does this and stores the resulting object program in a new file. Despite the name a linkage editor bears no resemblance to an editor.

ASSEMBLER

An *assembler* is like a compiler, but it is a much simpler and cheaper program because it translates from a *low-level*, or *assembly*, language. This is a language similar to the computer's machine code but with a few simple refinements. Like a machine code an assembly language can only be used for a particular make of microprocessor.

DEBUGGER

Debugging means trying to find and cure bugs in a program you have written. If you have a program that has been compiled or assembled (but not a program being interpreted) you can use a *debugger* as an aid.

It is not usually a separate program, but a facility included in the computer's monitor. When you type the command to load and run your program you give it an extra parameter that means the debugger is to come into operation. Now when your program is running it will stop after each instruction, and you can type commands to make the debugger display and alter data and instructions currently in memory. This is often a great help, but of course it's the object program, in machine code, that is running, and you need at least a vague understanding of the machine code to follow it.

4
APPLICATIONS

1. Introduction

The purpose of this chapter is to illustrate the kinds of things a computer program may do for you, the kind of price you will pay and the kind of computer you will need for particular types of application. It will do so by describing a number of actual packages currently on the market.

Really a chapter on what you might buy a computer for ought to be the first thing in the book. But this chapter goes into some practical detail, and so needs to use terms explained in the first three chapters. So it was thought better to leave this chapter until now, but include in chapter 2 some brief examples of uses.

The programs described here were chosen to cover as wide a range as possible, both in price and in application. They are of course only a tiny sample of the great many on the market. They come from a small number of software houses, for the purely practical reason that these were the firms the author of this book was able to visit for demonstrations. Thanks are due to these firms for their assistance (they are listed in the acknowledgements at the front of the book).

Because any software house tends to concentrate on one type of machine, all these programs are either for a large micro-computer with a CP/M operating system, or for a Sinclair ZX81. These are in any case excellent examples of very popular types of large and small computers respectively.

Sections 3 and 4 describe briefly how you load a program on a computer with the CP/M operating system and on a Sinclair ZX81. Of the remaining sections you need read only those that interest you; they illustrate the following applications:

5) integrated business system
6) payroll for a large micro-computer
7) data management system
8) financial planning
9) payroll for a small micro-computer
10) budget
11) finance programs for home and small business
12) fantasy game
13) simple games

2. Some common terms

This section explains some terms used in this chapter.

To *enter*	To enter data, a command, or a program means to type it into a computer. People also say a computer "enters" a program, meaning the computer starts executing it.
To *edit*	To amend the contents of a file using an editor or similar.
Main menu, *master menu,* *sub-menu*	In some programs, when you select an option (see below) from the menu another menu appears giving more choices. The first menu is called the main menu or master menu, and any others are called sub-menus.
Option	The alternatives given in a menu are called options.
To *select*	To select an option from a menu means to type the number displayed alongside it, so the computer will carry out that option.
* and /	The usual multiplication sign on computers is an asterisk, and the usual division sign is an oblique.

3. Using CP/M

If you have the CP/M operating system you probably have a large micro-computer, which you use for big programs for business. As chapter 3 said, when you buy a program it will come on a floppy disc, and you copy it onto your hard disc if you have one, or onto a floppy of your own containing a copy of CP/M.

On a computer with CP/M the disc drives are known as drive A, drive B and so on. This is how you refer to them in commands. If you have twin floppy drives, then to load a program you put the disc containing it and a copy of CP/M onto drive A; you probably have your data files on another disc, and this you put on drive B. If you have a hard disc drive your one disc is probably permanently on the drive.

You then simply type the name of the program. This is in effect a command to CP/M to load it. The loading takes a few seconds, and the program then starts running.

If the program needs to be executed by an interpreter, you type the name of the interpreter and then the name of the program.

4. Using a Sinclair ZX81

With a Sinclair ZX81 you keep programs on a domestic tape recorder. Programs you buy come on cassette. Program files have names like on a disc, and to load a program you type the "load" command, giving the name of the file. If you position the tape just before the program you want you can in fact miss the name out; the computer will load the first program it comes to on the tape.

You put the cassette in the tape recorder, rewind it to before the start of the program, and type the command

LOAD "..."

to load it; you put the name of the program (which will be given on an instruction sheet) between the quotes, where we have put "...". You start the tape just before you hit the newline key, as the return key is called on a ZX81. If you don't need to give the name of the program you simply type

LOAD " "

As always when loading from a domestic tape recorder, you may have to experiment with the volume control on the tape recorder to find the right setting for the computer to receive the program successfully.

The ZX81 has a Basic interpreter in ROM, so the interpreter automatically starts running when you switch on. Commands you type are executed by the interpreter. Once you have loaded a program you then type

RUN

to run it. Some programs though start running automatically.

The ZX81 does not use data files, and all information that a program keeps is part of the program. So when you use a program to update some information you are updating the program in memory, and you then need to save this copy of the program on a new tape, to use next time. After running the program you put a blank tape in the tape recorder, and rewind it to the beginning. You then type

SAVE ". . ."

putting between the quotes the name you want to give the program. Here you must not miss the name out.

Some programs include an option which makes the program store itself onto the tape. You use this instead of the SAVE command.

5. An integrated business system

On one computer a business will certainly keep several master files, each with programs to maintain it. Sometimes an update to one implies that an update is needed to another; for example entering an order into an orders file – which will make the computer print such things as delivery note and invoice – implies that the items on the order should be subtracted from the stock file.

This is one reason why people sometimes, instead of buying one package for invoicing, one for stock control, and so on, buy one package that includes all the programs needed to maintain all their files. The programs are designed to work together, so that a change in one file automatically causes the necessary changes to others. There is also the convenience of buying all your principal programs in one go, from one supplier. Such a package is often called an *integrated business system*. Sometimes you can buy the computer itself together with the package.

As an example this section will describe a package called ISBS-F, produced by a software house called Graffcom Systems. It consists of seven programs, which Graffcom call "modules" of the system. The modules are as follows.

1) Payroll   Maintains a file of your employees, and prints payslips, summaries, lists of coins and notes needed, etc.

2) Stock control	Maintains a file of items you stock, with stock levels; prints stock reports, orders to suppliers, etc.
3) Order entry and invoicing	Maintains a file of current orders, prints acknowledgements, invoices, sales analyses, etc.
4) Company purchases	Maintains a file of invoices received, details of supplier accounts, VAT details, prints a purchases ledger, cash requirements forecast, etc.
5) Company sales	Maintains a file of your sales invoices, details of customer accounts, VAT details, prints a sales ledger, debit and credit notes, lists of aged debtors, etc.
6) Name and address	Maintains a file of the names and addresses of all your customers, suppliers, etc.
7) General accounting	Prints standard financial statements and audit trails, petty cash analyses, etc, based on the files maintained by the other modules.

Each module can be bought and used separately – they cost a few hundred pounds each – or several can be used together. These modules separately are good examples of what you would get if you bought separate packages, so the Payroll module is used as an example in section 6.

ISBS-F is for a computer with two floppy disc drives. There is another version, called ISBS-W, for a computer with a hard disc. It is very similar.

For some of the modules you need special stationery such as payslips, invoice forms, etc. The software house or dealer can sell you these if you wish. For some forms, such as P11s, the approval of the Inland Revenue was needed, and has been obtained. If you use special stationery in the form of cheques you should ask your bank's approval, and the software house or dealer will arrange for the stationery to be printed with your own logo. You should keep any that are not used; in using any continuous stationery some is wasted in lining up the paper in the printer, and an auditor may ask what has happened to the missing numbers.

This package is for a computer with the CP/M operating system. The package is written in a dialect of Basic called *CBasic*. This dialect of Basic is not interpreted, but it is compiled into an intermediate code as explained in chapter 3, so to use the package your computer must have system software for running CBasic.

6. Payroll for a large micro-computer

The payroll package this section describes is the payroll module of the ISBS-F integrated business system described in section 5.

When you buy the payroll module the dealer does an initialisation run, in which he *formats* the master file. He stores some information about it on the disc you will keep it on, in effect creating it, though with no records. Among other things he stores a note of the maximum number of records (there'll be one for each employee) you will want it to hold. The maximum you can have is 500. He will also store your company name and, since payroll information is confidential, a password which you will have to type every time you use the program.

For this module there is a program updating service. When nationally fixed data, such as tax bands, changes, the software house automatically send you a new version of the module. This service costs an annual fee.

With the discs in the appropriate drives you type:

CRUN PAY

which is the command to CP/M to load and execute the CBasic system which in turn is to load and execute the program called PAY. All this takes only a few seconds, and then the program is running and displays

GRAFFCOM BUSINESS SYSTEMS
ISBS-F PAYROLL MODULE
In use by J. Bloggs Groceries

where the name in the last line is of course your own company name. (Unlike many programs ISBS-F sometimes uses lower case letters.) It then displays a request for you to type the password. When you have done so the above title disappears from the screen and the following menu appears:

1. Employee maintenance
2. Payroll log maintenance
3. Special deductions
4. Pay method analysis
5. Payroll run
6. Year end maintenance
7. System maintenance
8. Generate next payroll disc
9. Security copies

This is the list of options, or things the program can do, and you type the number of the option you now want. Let us suppose you are running the program for the first time and want to put details of your employees in the file. You type 1, and the menu disappears and is replaced by another, called a sub-menu:

1. Add employee
2. Change employee details
3. Delete employee

Since you want to add an employee, you type 1. A form appears on the screen with spaces, or fields, for all the details that go in an employee's record; details such as personnel number, name, NI details, tax code, department or cost centre, bank account number, bank sorting code, bank address, whether paid hourly, weekly or monthly, whether paid by cash, cheque or credit transfer, and so on.

You fill in the form, typing one employee's details. As you complete one field the cursor automatically moves on to the next. You will probably leave some fields blank; if he's to be paid by cash for example you won't need his bank details. You simply press the return key and the cursor moves to the next field. Where you need to specify one of several alternatives – how he's paid, for example – you type a one character code. These codes are given in the manual for the module.

When you complete the last field the form vanishes; the information in it has been made into a record in the payroll file.

Henceforth you can use option 1 (1st menu) to update an employee's details, or merely as an inquiry facility to display them. Some of the other options enable you to print the following reports:

1) Complete list of employees by name and personnel

number, with relevant personal information from the file.

2) A payroll log report, showing all movements during the last payroll run.

3) Payslips, incorporating your company name and a breakdown of net pay.

4) Bank Giro slips (if you pay people by credit transfer).

5) Year end reports, giving a summary of all details, together with P11/P60s.

6) A personnel report, giving employee details with length of service.

7) A bank money list, giving a breakdown of what coins and notes you need from the bank for the pay packets.

8) An overtime report, listing the overtime hours worked by each employee.

7. Data Management System

A *data management system* is a set of programs for general-purpose record keeping. Unlike other programs it is not designed to keep a particular master file. Instead you can use it to keep all your master files; you set up a new master file by describing to the system what data you want to keep in the file. You can type inquiries as normal, for the system to answer with data from the files, and you can print reports in a standard format or in a format you specify.

An example of a data management system is a package called DMS, produced by software house Compsoft. It costs a few hundred pounds and is for computers with the CP/M operating system. You need disc drives, at least 48K of memory for user programs (remember that the operating system takes up some memory) and a video that can display 80 characters on a line; many videos only have space for 40. There is also a version available for the Commodore Pet.

DMS is designed to be used by secretaries or clerks, and you describe to it in plain English what you want. For a master file that you want it to keep you type a *file description*, describing the fields to go in each record (each record in a file will have the same layout of fields), and it saves this description in a small file of its own. You can then type data to be put in records in the file.

You can specify what reports you want the system to print. You can make the system look up all the records in a file that meet certain criteria; for example, in a payroll file you might want to find every record in which a field called DATE-OF-BIRTH contains a date more than 65 years before today's date. You can also make the system sort the records in a file into a particular order. You would normally do these things to get the selected or sorted records printed on a report. DMS will save the *selections* and *sort descriptions* that you type in small files too, so you can use them again without having to re-type them.

You can also type a calculation to be done on selected records. You would do this to up-date the records. For example, say you award a general pay rise of 10% to everyone in your Sales Department. In each employee's record in your payroll master file you presumably have fields, called, say, SALARY and DEPT, showing the employee's salary and department. You up-date the file, specifying that, in each record in which DEPT contains the characters "SALES", the amount in SALARY is to be increased by 10%.

Having loaded CP/M you type DMS to load and run the package. It takes only a few seconds to load, and then starts running and displays the following menu:

A: CONFIGURE	B: CREATE	C: KEY	D: SORT
E: SELECT	F: REDEFINE	G: MASK	H: REPORT
I: LABEL	J: BROWSE	K: PROCESS	L: LINK
M: COPY	N: RESET	O: BACK-UP	X: EXIT

This is the list of things the system can do. If at this point you press the space bar on the keyboard the menu disappears and a brief explanation of what each of the options is for appears. Pressing the space bar again brings the menu back.

You select option A if you want to describe to DMS what kind of video and printer you have; normally you do this only once, on getting DMS, and the dealer will probably help you.

To create a new master file you select option B. A message

Loading program, please wait

appears on the screen, while the program that carries out this option is loaded. (Unlike many programs DMS uses lower-case letters.) Then after a few seconds the program displays some questions about the file you want to create. You type your answer after the ">" at the end of each question. The manual describes the form in which you type the answer to each question. In the following example, adapted with permission from the User's Guide that Compsoft provide with the package, answers you might give are shown after the ">":

> Enter date > 21JAN82
> Do you wish to base this file on a previous file definition? > N
> Enter drive on which the file is to be created > B
> Enter new file name > STAFF
> Enter description of the file > Personnel records

This tells DMS you want to create a file called STAFF on the disc on drive B. The description "Personnel records" will be stored in the file to be displayed or printed when you use the file.

Since you said you did not want the file to be based on an existing file definition, the system asks you to describe what information you will want to put in the file. It asks you about the fields to go in a record. Answers you might give are:

> Enter heading for field number 1 > NAME
> Enter field type > C
> Enter field length > 30

This tells the system the length of the first field in each record, the type of data you will keep in it (it could be a number, a string of characters, or a date), and the heading to be printed on reports above the column showing data from this field.

When you have described all the fields to go in a record of the file you type *END, which tells DMS you have finished. DMS then creates the file you have described, though as yet it has no data in it, and then the menu reappears.

To put data in the file you select option C, the "key" option. DMS displays the file definition, which is a list of the names of the fields in a record, and their lengths and the type of data each can hold. You can then type information for each field, and DMS will create a record in the file. In this way you create as many records as you need to hold all your information.

The first field in a record is called its key field, and you can get the data in a record displayed by typing the data you know is in its key field; in the present example the key field is NAME, intended to hold an employee's name, and so you can get an employee's details displayed by typing his name. This is how you do an inquiry, and also how you update the details in an employee's record; you display his record in this way and then type the changes you want to make.

To get the records in a file sorted into a particular order you choose option D, and type a sort description, explained in the User Guide. A sort description describes into what order the records are to be sorted. Similarly, to select only some of the records for inclusion on a report you choose option E and type a selection.

A report can be produced using the *standard report writer* or the *user-defined report writer*. To use the standard report writer you select option H, whereupon a sub-menu is displayed and you select option A from the sub-menu. With this option the layout of the report is standard; normally every field in each record is shown, in a column with the field heading at the top. You can, though, specify that only certain fields from each record are to be shown. To get the user-defined report writer you select option H, and then when the sub-menu appears you select option B. With this option you type a detailed description of the layout of the report you want.

8. Financial planning

Financial planning typically consists of deciding or estimating such things as production levels, sales, prices and expenditure over the next few months, and working out what you can expect cash flow and profits to be as a consequence. Often you want to try out different sets of figures and see how the results compare, so you can decide – for figures such as production levels and prices, which you decide rather than having to estimate – which figures to put into practice. Even if working out these cash flows and profits is fairly simple, doing it repeatedly by hand with different sets of figures is very time-consuming.

With a financial planning program on a computer you store in a file a description of the calculation the program is to do, and several alternative sets of figures. It will then display or print the cash flow forecast worked out from each set of figures. This takes only a few moments, so you can quickly compare the alternatives and choose the best plan to follow.

One example of a financial planning package is Fastplan, produced by an international computer services company called Comshare. It costs £395, and is sold on floppy discs, for a computer with a CP/M operating system, at least 56K of memory, and two disc drives each with a capacity of at least 250K. As well as plans and *consolidations* (combining figures for different parts of the company) it can do *what-if questions*, where you change one quantity and the program works out how the results will change, and *goal-seeking problems*, where you type what results you want to achieve and the computer works out what figures you will have to work to.

To try out a plan you use Fastplan to create several files. One is called the *model file*, and contains a description of the calculation to be done; the *model* as it is called. The others contain the alternative sets of figures, and are called the *data files*.

Having loaded CP/M you type FASTPLAN. After a few seconds the program has been loaded and starts running, and it displays the following menu:

1. Edit model or data file
2. Data file column update
3. Calculation
4. Print results
5. What-if questions
6. Backwards iteration (goal seeking)
7. Set up screen control codes

Select (or END) . . .

The message at the end tells you to type the number of the option you want to use, or type END if you want to finish with Fastplan and return to CP/M. Option 7 is for configuring Fastplan, and you are unlikely to use it after the first run, which the dealer may help you with.

To create the model file for your calculation you type 1. This brings into action an editor built into Fastplan, which displays some questions asking whether you want to create a new file or amend an existing one, and whether it will be a model file or a data file. You type replies indicating that you are going to create a model file (the Fastplan manual explains the exact form of these replies) and you type a name to be given to the file. You can then type the description of the calculation, in a simple notation given in the manual. The following is an example adapted, with Comshare's permission, from that manual:

```
10 TITLE MONTHLY PROFIT FORECAST
20 COLUMNS JAN, FEB, MAR, APR
30 PRICE
40 UNIT SALES
50 REVENUE = R30 * R40
60 COSTS
70 PROFIT = R50 - R60
80 CUM PROFIT = CUM R70
```

Remember that the purpose of this calculation is to produce a profit forecast, showing the profitability of your company over the next few months. This model says the title at the top of the forecast is to be "MONTHLY PROFIT FORE-CAST", and that there are to be four columns, headed JAN, FEB, MAR, APR, and six rows, labelled PRICE, UNIT SALES, REVENUE, COSTS, PROFIT, AND CUM PROFIT. This particular forecast obviously concerns one product only. For each column Fastplan is to read the price, unit sales and costs from a data file, and it is to work out the revenue, profit and cumulative profit from these. It is to work out the revenue as price times sales, the profit as revenue minus costs, and the cumulative profit by adding together the profits in the months so far.

You are not compelled to work in monthly periods on these forecasts. All the program knows is that your report is to have several columns, showing the forecast figures for several consecutive periods. It is up to you to decide whether to enter monthly or weekly figures or whatever you choose, and to give appropriate headings for the columns.

As with any editor you can now make corrections to what you have typed. The lines have numbers so you can indicate to the editor which lines you want to change, and so that lines can refer to one another. The line numbers go up in tens so you can insert a line by giving it a number in between those of the lines it is to go between.

When you have finished typing the model you type
SWITCH to show you are now going to type a data file. Again
you type a name to be given to the file. Now the editor,
referring to the model file, asks you to type the data the model
requires. With the above model, the program would ask you
for the expected price, unit sales and costs for each of the four
months. The prompts it would give, together with examples
of what you might reply, are as follows:

```
PRICE              > C 15
UNIT SALES         > L 500 50
COSTS              > 5000 5000 6000 6000
```

C 15 is short for "constant 15", and by this you mean the price
will be £15 during each of the four months. L stands for *linear*
(in a straight line), and by this you mean you expect the unit
sales to be 500 in the first month increasing each month by 50.
These abbreviations and others you can use are given in the
manual. Where you give four figures (as for the COSTS) they
are simply the figures for the different months.

Now that you have created the model file and a data file to
go with it you type END, and the menu re-appears on the
screen. Now you can select option 3, and the program will do
the calculation and display or print the forecast. This takes it
only a few seconds. With the example above you would get:

MONTHLY PROFIT FORECAST

		JAN	FEB	MAR	APR
30	PRICE	15	15	15	15
40	UNIT SALES	500	550	600	650
50	REVENUE	7,500	8,250	9,000	9,750
60	COSTS	5,000	5,000	6,000	6,000
70	PROFIT	2,500	3,250	3,000	3,750
80	CUM PROFITS	2,500	5,750	8,750	12,500

Thus you have a forecast of profits, based on what you
intend the price of the product to be, and what you estimate
your sales and costs will be, over the next four months. You
can now type in more data files, or amend the one you have
just used, to see how things would be with different figures.

Even with the simple model in this example using a financial planning program is quicker than doing the calculation

over and over by hand. You can have models as complicated as you like, and can build up a number of model files to cover different parts of your business. The biggest *matrix* (table) you can have is 60 columns by 300 rows.

There are also facilities to consolidate as many data files as required, and to have commands stored in a command file. Unfortunately there is no space here to describe how you use these, or how you use the what-if and goal-seeking facilities of Fastplan.

9. Payroll for a small micro-computer

A software house called Hilderbay sell a payroll program for use on a Sinclair ZX81 with at least 16K of memory. It is sold on a tape cassette by mail order at £25, and can be used for up to 30 employees.

When you load the program it automatically starts running, and displays ENTER CODE. You type a password (this password is given in the manual, but there is a way you can change it). When you have typed the password the following menu appears:

> SELECT ONE OF:
> 0:   SAVE RESULTS ON TAPE.
> 1:   DO AN EMPLOYEE'S PAY.
> 2:   SUMMARY FOR ALL EMPLOYEES.
>
> 9:   SET MONTH/WEEK NUMBER.
> X: STOP (OPTIONAL)

The ZX81 does not use data files. All the employee records are kept in the program file, so when you have loaded the program they are all in memory. The program file as supplied contains 30 records, but the fields in them are blank, except that there are a few fictitious entries for you to practise with.

To add an employee to the file you select option 1. The program searches the file for an unused record, indicated by a blank name field, and displays the contents on the screen as a form. Unless this record previously belonged to an employee now deleted all the fields will be blank. You then fill in the form with the new employee's data. To change an employee's data you select option 1 and then type the employee's name, or enough of it to distinguish him from others. Again the contents of his record are displayed as the form on the screen, and you can type changes.

The form is as follows:

```
1:   NAME =
2:   TAX CODE =
3:   NI CODE =

MONTH IS 6. AT END OF MONTH 5:
4:   GROSS PAY TO DATE =
5:   TAX PAID TO DATE =
6:   REGULAR PAY =
7:   PRE-TAX CHANGES =
8:   POST-TAX CHANGES =

RUN = R: NO CHANGES – COMPUTE PAY
RETURN = Y: RETURN TO MASTER MENU
NEXT = N: NEXT EMPLOYEE
COPY = Z: COPY
G: GROSS UP GIVEN NET PAY
```

You use this like a menu. You type the number of the field you want to change, and the cursor moves to just after the equals sign on that line, so you can type the new data. When you have filled in what you want you select one of the options at the bottom. To delete an employee after he has left (you have to keep him on file for several years, for tax purposes) you change the name field to a blank; the program will recognise this as meaning "deleted". After adding or deleting an employee or changing details you would type "NEXT" to do another employee or "Y" to get the main menu displayed again.

To indicate that an employee is paid by the hour you enter the "regular pay" as Ø. The program then displays a message asking you to type the employee's hourly rate.

You also use option 1 to print a payslip. When you have typed an employee's name and the form appears, you press the key marked "run" on the computer. The program will display a payslip for the employee. You can copy the details by hand onto your firm's payslip form, or if you have a printer (Sinclair sell an electrostatic one, which prints on a roll of silvered paper) you can make the program print the payslip as on the screen.

The program should be used either entirely for weekly-paid employees or entirely for monthly-paid employees. If you have both you should use two copies of the program and run them separately. You use option 9 (normally once only) to tell the program whether you will use it for monthly or weekly pay. This doesn't affect the calculations, but controls certain safeguards. Each payday, that is, each time you run the program, you use option 9 to tell the program the current week or month number, and it checks that, according to the file, each employee has been paid up to the previous week or month.

You can also make the program display or print summaries, and, an unusual feature, you can enter a net sum you have paid to an employee and the program will work out what the gross sum, tax and deductions must have been.

When you have finished a weekly or monthly run, you save the program from memory onto a new tape, as described in section 4. This program has the up-to-date employee file in it, and you use this version for your next run.

10. Budget

Budget is the name of a program sold by software house Hilderbay. It is sold on a tape cassette by mail order for £15 and is for a Sinclair ZX81 with at least 16K of memory. It helps with planning and keeping track of expenditure in the home or a small business.

When you load the program it automatically starts running and prompts you to enter the name of the month whose budget you want to work out. You type the first three letters of the name, and then the program displays the following menu:

    0:   SAVE DATA ON TAPE.
    1:   ENTER/EDIT PLANNED EXPENDITURE.
    2:   ENTER/EDIT ACTUAL EXPENSES.
    3:   COMPARE EXPENSES WITH PLAN.
    4:   EXAMINE A PREVIOUS MONTH.
    5:   PLOT GRAPH.
    6:   TOTALS TO DATE.

7: CHANGE CURRENT MONTH.
8: LIST/ADD/DELETE HEADING.

Say you want to type your planned expenditure for the month. You type 1, the menu disappears and the program prompts you to type. You can type several quantities, each with a heading and a description. The heading is so you can have in effect several budgets, for different departments for example. The headings you can have are stored in the program; you can change them using option 8. When you have typed all the figures the program displays them as a column; it would show for one heading, for example:

```
1982 MAY
HIGH STREET BRANCH
     0.00  C/F
    45.00  TRANSPORT
     5.00  SUNDRIES

    50.00  TOTAL
```

You can store the figures by saving the program from memory onto a new tape, as described in section 4, and using this version of the program next time. You type the actual expenditure for a month in the same way as planned expenditure. Then you can compare planned with actual. You reply to the menu by typing 3, and the program displays the differences between planned and actual expenditure for each heading, as in the following example:

	Actual	Budget	Diff.
HIGH STREET BRANCH	45.87	50.00	—4.13
ROSE LANE BRANCH	106.45	100.00	6.45
TOTAL	152.32	150.00	2.32

Using option 5 you can make the program show your expenditure over the year so far as a bar chart.

11. Finance programs for home and small business

Financial Pack 1 is a cassette of three programs for everyday financial calculations sold by software house Hilderbay. it is sold on a tape cassette by mail order at £8 and is for a

Sinclair ZX81 computer with at least 16K of memory. This section will describe two of the programs.

MORTGAGE

With this program you type details of a mortgage and it works out the state the mortgage will have reached after each instalment. When you load and run the program it displays on the screen the following explanation:

4 IMPORTANT QUANTITIES: AMOUNT OF LOAN (PRINCIPAL), INSTALMENT, NUMBER OF INSTALMENTS, INTEREST. ANY ONE OF THESE CAN BE COMPUTED FROM THE OTHER 3

ENTER 3 OF THE ITEMS REQUESTED, FOLLOWING EACH WITH A "NEWLINE". (ENTER NEWLINE ONLY FOR THE OMITTED ITEM.)

THE FOURTH WILL BE CALCULATED.

ANSWER ANY OF THE QUESTIONS WITH "HELP" IF YOU LIKE.

The program then prompts you to type in the four quantities required to describe the mortgage, and you type any three of them – the program will work out the fourth. When you are asked for the one you intend to omit you simply press the newline key, the ZX81's equivalent of return. If you answer HELP to any prompt the program displays an explanation of what is required. When you have entered three quantities the program displays all four quantities together.

You can then type the number of an instalment and the program will display the remaining balance, total interest paid so far, amount of the instalment that is interest, and total amortised (paid off), at that instalment. Alternatively you can make the program print a table showing this information for every instalment. The program is useful if you are thinking of starting a mortgage. By running the program repeatedly with different sets of figures you can see quickly how small changes in payments will affect the duration; the effect can be considerable.

Banks and building societies have different ways of calculating the monthly repayments on a mortgage, and so repayments may be slightly different on a building society mortgage than on a bank one at the same rate of interest. The program can work either way, so you can use it to work out either kind of mortgage.

VAT

With this program you can type prices exclusive of Value Added Tax (VAT), and the program will work out the VAT to be added; alternatively you can type them inclusive of VAT, and the program will work out what part of each price is VAT.

When you load and run the program it displays on the screen the following explanation:

ENTER ITEMS OF EXPENDITURE AS THE AMOUNT, FOLLOWED BY A LETTER AND THE VAT PERCENTAGE, IF NOT THE STANDARD RATE (15%).

TO CHANGE THE STANDARD RATE, STOP THE RUN, ENTER "1 LET VAT = 8" (SAY), THEN NEWLINE. THEN SAVE THE MODIFIED PROGRAM ON TAPE.

THE LETTER "I" IS USED FOR VAT-INCLUSIVE PRICES, "X" FOR EX-VAT PRICES. IF NO LETTER IS ENTERED, "I" IS ASSUMED.

ENTER "END" AFTER LAST ITEM.

Then the program prompts you to type, and you type in a column of prices you want analysed. As the explanation says, if you type "I" after a price this means you have typed it including VAT and you want the program to work out the VAT-less price and the VAT; if you type "X" this means you have typed it excluding VAT and you want the VAT and the total price worked out. If you do not type any letter it is as if you had typed "I".

After each price you type the VAT-rate the program is to assume. If you don't it assumes 15%, the standard rate when the program was written. However you can change the program; if the standard rate were to change to 8% you would load the program and type

1 LET VAT = 8

which is a statement in Basic and will actually replace the first statement of the program in memory. You would then save the program from memory on a new tape, and henceforth use this updated version.

When you have typed all the prices you want analysed you type END and the program will then display them in columns, with totals, as in the following example:

4.35	0.65	5.00	15
100.00	8.00	108.00	8
50.00	6.00	56.00	12
35.71	4.29	40.00	12
190.06	18.94	209.00	TOTALS

where the first column is the ex-VAT price, the second is the VAT, the third is the price including VAT, and the fourth is the VAT rate. This program would no doubt be very useful in a small business such as a shop.

12.   Fantasy game

In chapter 2 (page 20) we briefly describe fantasy games. An example of a fantasy game is 3D Monster Maze, sold by J. K. Greye Software by mail order for £4.95. It is sold on cassette, and is for a Sinclair ZX81 computer with at least 16K of memory.

This game is simpler and shorter to play than most fantasy games, but is unusual in that it shows 3-dimensional views of what is going on. Most such games show on the screen a diagrammatic bird's eye view of the maze (or whatever) you are in, with symbols such as asterisks to show where the monsters are and where you are. Some just display messages describing what's around you. A few programs, though, of which 3D Monster Maze is one, display what you would actually see, with perspective to make the scenes look 3-dimensional. As chapter 2 said, the pictures a computer displays are very stylised, but they still bring the game to life.

Like most fantasy games, this program is *real-time*. That is, it doesn't wait while you make up your mind on your next move; things are going on all the time, as they would be in real life, and you have to think quickly. In this game you are lost in a maze, and somewhere in the maze is a prehistoric monster, a Tyrannosaurus Rex, who is wandering round looking for you with a view to lunch. You move around the maze looking for the one exit and trying to avoid the monster. On the right of the screen the program displays your score, which measures how many paces you have taken in the maze.

With the cassette comes an instruction sheet, which tells you how to load the program and describes briefly the idea of the game, but detailed instructions are displayed on the screen when you run the program. This is a big program to load from tape, and takes about four minutes to playback and load. When it has been loaded the program displays:

ANYONE THERE?
WELL PRESS SOMETHING THEN

and then waits till you press a key. You can press any key, with the obvious exceptions of shift (which by itself wouldn't do anything) and break, the ZX81's equivalent of reset. You are then introduced to the game by a master of ceremonies; on the left of the screen appears a picture of a clown, and on the right appear instructions on playing the game. These instructions scroll up, and from time to time they stop, the clown bows, and a message appears asking whether you want more instructions, and telling you which keys you can press to reply. If you press the key meaning you need no more instructions the game starts.

You now find yourself looking down a long corridor, with white floor and ceiling, black walls, and grey corridors opening off the side. On the right of the screen is the word SCORE, where the program will display your score throughout the game. Below the picture is displayed some hint of what the dinosaur is up to, such as:

HE IS LYING IN WAIT
or HE IS LOOKING FOR YOU
or HE IS BEHIND YOU

By pressing the 5, 7 and 8 keys you move around the maze. You press 5 to turn left, 8 to turn right, and 7 to move forward. These keys were chosen simply because they're in convenient positions on the keyboard. You don't have to hit newline before a key has effect; in fact you can hold a key down and it will keep you moving.

As you move, the picture on the screen changes, as the walls of the corridor flash past or you turn to face a different way. The monster is wandering around too, and the hint displayed of what he's doing changes from time to time. When you come face to face with him you see him striding up the corridor towards you. You must quickly turn and run away, otherwise the last picture you see is of his teeth filling the screen. Then appears a message saying he's got you and asking if you want to try again.

While you are playing, the computer keeps score on the right of the screen. For each step that you take in the maze it adds 5 to your score. Somewhere there is an exit, which appears as a pulsating pattern on a wall at the end of a corridor. When you go through it you are safe and the program adds a bonus of 200 to your score. You can press a key to indicate you want to play again.

To play again after escaping or after the dinosaur has got you, you don't need to load again. The program is of course still in memory, and hitting a key makes it execute again.

When you load the program, or start a new game after escaping from the maze, the program decides at random what the layout of the maze will be. This means you get a different maze each time.

13. Simple games

On page 20 of chapter 2 we mentioned video games. An example of video games and other simple games is Gamestape 1, a cassette containing ten games sold by J. K. Greye Software by mail order for £1.95. It is for a basic Sinclair ZX81 computer, which has only 1K of memory for programs to fit in. This section will describe two of the games.

GUILLOTINE

This game is based on hangman, and needs two players. When you have loaded the program it displays a message asking you to type a word. One player does so, the other not looking. The second player then has to guess the word. At the top of the screen the program displays a row of dots, as many as there are letters in the word. The player guessing types a letter. If that letter happens to be in the word, the dot at the appropriate position changes to the letter. If not part of a guillotine appears on the screen. This goes on until either the player has completed the word correctly or the guillotine is finished. The guillotine consists of just two lines representing uprights, which the program takes several goes to complete, and cross-pieces at top and bottom. The last thing added is a small circle at the bottom, representing a head. If the player gets the next go wrong a line representing the blade comes sliding down and the head disappears.

ASTEROIDS

In this game you can imagine you are piloting a spaceship through a region of space full of asteroids. You have to see how long you can keep going before hitting one of them.

The program displays a bird's eye view of the scene. Your spaceship is represented by a U and each asteroid by an O. Your spaceship leaves behind a trail of *'s, which give the illusion it is moving down the screen, although really it's the asteroids that are moving up. As long as you keep any key pressed the U moves to the left, otherwise it moves to the right. When you eventually collide with an asteroid the program displays something like:

HI 60 Y/SC 60
AGAIN? (A/K)

meaning you scored 60, the highest score in your games so far is 60, and you should press any key if you want to play again. These abbreviations are necessary for the program to fit in the 1K memory. If you do press a key the game begins again.

The highest score so far is stored as part of the program. On the tape you receive from the software house it is of course Ø, and so whenever you load from this tape your highest score before your first game will always be zero. But you can if you want save your highest score from one session to the next. When you've finished playing you save the program from memory onto a blank tape, and next time you load the program you load from this tape. This program will be just the same as on the original tape but with your highest score from the previous session stored in it.

5
ABOUT PROGRAMMING

1. Introduction

The rest of the book is for people wondering whether to take up programming. It is not a complete course. People usually learn programming by learning a programming language, and for this you would need a computer for trying out exercises; whereas this book is for someone who has no computer yet.

These chapters intend instead to make you familiar with what programming involves. They explain what all programs consist of, describe a method of writing programs, and illustrate some of the most popular languages. Thus you should feel able to decide whether to program, and able to approach a book on a programming language knowing what to expect.

If you plan to write short programs in Basic, do not be misled by the following into expecting it to be a big job. As earlier chapters said, you can buy a computer like the Sinclair ZX81 over the counter, take it home, plug it in, and, guided by the manual, be writing useful programs for simple tasks within hours. Much of the art of programming comes in writing large, complex programs (in Basic or any other language), and this part of the book explains things fully enough for people wanting to write such programs.

2. Notes about terminology

The word *translator* means an interpreter, compiler, or assembler, and to translate a program means to use one of these on it. In practice the words "translate" and "translator" are seldom used, but since here we are often talking about all three kinds of translator we will use these words frequently.

It is usual to distinguish between the *user* of a program, who runs it and has its services, and the programmer, who wrote it and so provided the service for the user. With a micro-computer the user and *programmer* are often the same person, but in these chapters we will say "the user does such-and-such" if we mean you do it when using the program rather than when writing it.

The following chapters use many words explained in earlier chapters. For convenient reference some of these words are listed again here.

LANGUAGES

High-level language	A programming language in which each instruction, called a statement, is a simple English-like phrase.
Low-level (or assembly) language	A programming language resembling a machine code, but with a few refinements for convenience.
Machine code	The language a computer can actually follow, in which each instruction is a number.

TRANSLATORS

Interpreter	A program that translates a program from a high-level language into machine code while the program is being executed, translating each statement in turn for the computer to execute immediately. Colloquially, people say the interpreter executes the program.
Compiler	A program that translates a program from a high-level language into machine code, and puts the translated program in a program file for the computer to execute later.
Assembler	Like a compiler, but for an assembly language.

OTHER SYSTEM PROGRAMS

Editor	A program that enables you to type a new program, to be put in a file ready for compiling or assembling.
Linkage editor	On large micro-computers, a program to join together object programs.
Debugger	A program (or part of the monitor) that makes your program stop after each instruction so you can follow it working.

MISCELLANEOUS	
Ø	Remember that people often cross their zeros.
To move	Remember that to move data or a program means to copy it; it does not imply that the original is deleted.
Source program	The program as written.
Object program	The translated program.
Bug	An error in a program.
To generate	A compiler or assembler is said to generate the object program from the source program.
Instruction set	The repertoire of machine code instructions a particular make of computer accepts; a feature in fact of its microprocessor.

3. Choosing a language

Hundreds of high-level languages have been invented over the years, but only a handful have become popular. For most computers there are interpreters or compilers available for only one or two high-level languages, so you should consider when choosing a computer what language you want to use. In theory you can write any program in any language, but each language has been designed for a particular kind of work (business say, or mathematics) and with the wrong language some programs are impracticable.

An assembly language reflects very closely the machine code of the computer it's for, so even if several are available for your machine they will be very similar. Since you control the computer in minute detail no kind of work will be less practicable than any other. Most programs will occupy less memory and take less time to execute than if written in a high level language; compilers produce long-winded object programs, and an interpreter must translate each statement every time the statement is executed. But an assembly language takes longer to learn, and programs take longer to write.

Most people learn just one programming language. If you use your computer for more than one kind of purpose – say some programs are for maintaining business files and others are for complex mathematical calculations – you might decide to learn more than one, provided the translators are available. Once you have been using a high-level language for a while you might learn your machine's assembly language, for programs that are awkward to write or slow to run using your original language.

Normally all the programs in a suite are written in the same language. This is not only for ease; the way a file is recorded on the tape or disc can depend on the language, so a program written in one language may not be able to read a file produced by a program written in another. But you could write parts of a suite in the machine's assembly language, where you have control of such things. You might do this if parts of a suite were proving impracticable in your high-level language.

Writing in machine code is so tedious as to be only of interest to people using a computer as a hobby. Obviously a computer manufacturer's system programmers, programming a new machine with no software, have to do it – but often the first thing they do is write themselves an assembler!

An important feature of a programming language is how easily you can read and understand a program written out on paper, when you are preparing it or amending it. Some years ago the ideal of most language designers was to make high-level languages as much like English as possible. The languages invented then were very successful; they are in widespread use and are easy for beginners to learn.

But however much like English a language is, no one can take in quickly a string of hundreds, perhaps thousands, of short statements. So some more recent languages are designed to make the general plan of a program easy to see. These are called *block-structured* languages, and although they look unfamiliar at first many people find them easy to use. Even if you don't use a block-structured language, it's easy and often useful to invent a simple one of your own for sketching rough notes for a program. This book does so in chapters 6 and 7.

A professional programmer usually goes on a one or two week course to learn a new language, and begins to feel competent after a few months' experience, in which he will have written several programs. If you teach yourself, from one of the many introductory text-books, then reading the book before getting a computer can only be a preliminary; you can only start learning when you have a computer to try exercises on. With a good book you can be writing small programs within a few hours. You can also learn a language from the manual you get with the translator, but these manuals are usually intended as reference books rather than introductions.

4. Examples of programming languages

Figures 1, 2, and 3 show one short program in three different languages. It is not intended that you should try to understand at this stage how this program works; it is shown merely to illustrate what a program looks like, and to emphasise the differences between languages. A short description is given of each version of the program, pointing out the main features of the language.

The program is very simple; when you run it it prompts you to type something, and when you do so it displays
            "YOU TYPED – "
followed by the text you typed. It then prompts you to type something again. This happens repeatedly until you type STOP. Then it finishes.

BASIC

Figure 1 shows the program in Basic. You usually type each statement on a new line. The number at the start of each line is called the *line number*. You use it when altering the program, to show the interpreter which line you want to alter. And you use it in the program so one statement can refer to another; for example line 60 tells the computer to go back to line 20 and continue from there.

```
10 REM DISPLAY A TEXT
20 PRINT "ENTER TEXT – "
30 INPUT A$
40 IF A$ = "STOP" THEN END
50 PRINT "YOU TYPED  – " + A$
60 GOTO 20
```

Fig. 1 – A short program in Basic

The word REM at the start of line 10 shows this line is a *remark*, or *comment*. It is only to explain, in plain English, to a person reading the program displayed on the screen or printed out on paper, what the program does; the computer will ignore it.

Line 30 tells the computer to stop and wait till the user has typed something. When it does so, and you type something and hit return, the computer will save what you type in memory, and will know it by the name A$; in this way you can give a name to an item of data (rather as in commands you can give a name to a file). Thereafter in the program (as in line 40) you can refer to it by this name.

The computer in fact gives the name to the place in memory where it is storing the item of data. This place is called a *variable* (because you could change the data in it), and its name is called a *variable name*. In Basic the "$" shows that the data is a text rather than a number.

The PRINT statements on lines 20 and 50 tell the computer to display on the screen what is between the quotes, and in line 50 to follow it by what is in the variable A$. The word END tells the computer to finish with the program and return to the interpreter.

COBOL

Figure 2 shows the same program in Cobol. A Cobol program is divided up into *divisions* and *sections* by *headers*. A comparison of short programs is very unfair to Cobol in that a program appears unnecessarily long, because every Cobol program must (in most, though not all, dialects) start with several lines of *documentary* statements, which like comments the computer ignores. In the big programs for which Cobol is designed this is very useful. Under the heading IDENTI-FICATION DIVISION you put who wrote the program, when, and so on; under the heading CONFIGURATION SECTION in the ENVIRONMENT DIVISION you describe the computer it's to be compiled on, the computer it's to be run on (usually the same of course) and so on. There are many other sections and statements you could include.

```
IDENTIFICATION DIVISION.
PROGRAM-ID. EXAMPLE.
AUTHOR. J. BLOGGS.
ENVIRONMENT DIVISION.
CONFIGURATION SECTION.
SOURCE-COMPUTER. APPLE-II.
OBJECT-COMPUTER. APPLE-II.
DATA DIVISION.
WORKING-STORAGE SECTION.
01 OUT-TEXT.
  02 FILLER  PICTURE X(12),
                VALUE "YOU TYPED - ".
  02 IN-TEXT PICTURE X(70).
PROCEDURE DIVISION.
*DISPLAY A TEXT
PROMPT.
      DISPLAY "ENTER TEXT -".
      ACCEPT IN-TEXT.
      IF IN-TEXT = "STOP" STOP RUN.
      DISPLAY OUT-TEXT.
      GO TO PROMPT.
```

Fig. 2 – The same program in Cobol

The program really starts with the part headed DATA DIVISION. Unlike in Basic you have to say in advance what variables – or *data items* as Cobol programmers call them – you will want to use, and describe them (give "pictures" of them). This is called *reserving* them, and you do it in the Data Division. Records read from, or to be written to, files (of which this program has none) are described in the *File Section*, and other data items in the *Working-storage Section*. These descriptions are called *data descriptions* or *declarations*.

We want a data item containing the 12 characters "YOU TYPED - ". It will have no name, as we will not refer to it directly; this is what *filler* means. Immediately after it in memory we want a data item 70 bytes long, called IN-TEXT. The program will put data in this while it is running. The two fields together are to be known as OUT-TEXT; the *level-numbers*, the numbers in front of each declaration, show that

IN-TEXT and the filler are *subordinate* to, or part of, OUT-TEXT.

The *Procedure Division* is where we write the actual instructions. Most lines start in column 8 (that is, 7 spaces from the start of the line) or 12. A line starting with an * in column 7 is a comment. The word PROMPT is called a *paragraph-name*; like a line number in Basic it names a point in the program so that another line can tell the computer to go to that line and continue from there. In making up a paragraph-name you try to make it remind you of what the lines after it do.

The ACCEPT and DISPLAY statements work like the INPUT and PRINT statements in Basic. In most dialects, though, each DISPLAY can only display one item, which is why we put the message "YOU TYPED – " next in memory to the data item storing what you typed, so we could refer to them as one item.

The statement STOP RUN is the equivalent of Basic's END; it tells the computer to finish with the program and return to the operating system (Cobol compilers generally need you to have an operating system, not just a monitor).

8080 ASSEMBLY LANGUAGE

Figure 3 shows the same program written in an assembly language for a computer with an Intel 8080 microprocessor and with the CP/M operating system. There is no point in explaining it in minute detail, but much of it will be clear when you have read this and subsequent chapters.

```
BOOT       EQU     0
BDOS       EQU     5
READF      EQU     10
PRINTF     EQU     9
CR         EQU     13
LF         EQU     10
*
           ORG     256
PROMP      MVI     C,PRINTF      ; PRINT THE PROMPT
           LXI     D,PROMPT
           CALL    BDOS
*
```

```
              LXI     H,INTEXT      ; CLEAR THE BUFFER
              MVI     C,69
CLEAR         MVI     M,32
              INX     H
              DCR     C
              JNZ     CLEAR
*
              MVI     C,READF       ; READ THE TEXT
              LXI     D,TXTCTL
              CALL    BDOS
*
              LDA     INTEXT        ; SEE IF IT IS 'STOP'
              CPI     'S'
              JNZ     REPLY
              LDA     INTEXT+1
              CPI     'T'
              JNZ     REPLY
              LDA     INTEXT+2
              CPI     'O'
              JNZ     REPLY
              LDA     INTEXT+3
              CPI     'P'
              JZ      BOOT
*

REPLY         MVI     C,PRINTF      ; PRINT THE REPLY
              LXI     D,MSG
              CALL    BDOS
              MVI     C, PRINTF
              LXI     D,INTEXT
              CALL    BDOS
              MVI     C,PRINTF
              LXI     D,NEWLIN
              CALL    BDOS
              JMP     PROMP
*
*
NEWLIN        DB      CR,LF,'$'
TXTCTL        DB      70,0

INTEXT        DS      70
              DB      '$'
PROMPT        DB      'ENTER TEXT -',CR,LF,'$'
MSG           DB      CR,LF,'YOU TYPED - $'
```

Figure 3 –The same program in 8080 Assembly language

Most of the instructions move data to and from small storage areas, called *registers*, in the central processor. Generally if you want to do arithmetic on an item of data (which includes comparing it to another) you have to put it in a register. The words written after the semi-colons are comments.

The first few lines give names to particular numbers that are to appear in the program. This is simply to make the program easier to read. The line ORG 256 tells the assembler whereabouts in the memory the program will start when it is loaded.

The last few lines declare data items, or *fields*, as assembly language programmers usually call them. INTEXT is a field 70 bytes long (DB stands for "define bytes") in which what you type will be saved. The fields that are to be displayed have special codes in them to make the screen scroll up (CR and LF), and to show where each field ends ($).

The names PROMPT, CLEAR and REPLY are called *labels*, and serve the same purpose as the line numbers in Basic and paragraph-names in Cobol.

The lines CALL BDOS call the operating system to do jobs like reading into the memory what is typed and writing a line of text onto the screen. When you type STOP the line JZ BOOT makes the program finish; it tells the computer to go to whatever instruction is at the start of the memory (we defined BOOT to mean Ø). This is where the operating system starts. So the computer will return to the start of the operating system, as if the user had done a bootstrap.

MACHINE CODE

If this program were to be written in machine code it would be exactly as in the assembly language, but with numbers instead of words and with no spacing or comments to make it more readable.

5.   Stages in producing a program

In producing a program you go through several stages:
1) designing it
2) *coding* it
3) typing it in
4) translating it

5) testing it.
Coding means actually writing the program, in your programming language.

Since any program has errors when first tested, then come:
6) debugging it
7) correcting it
8) translating it again
9) testing it again.
You usually go through these four stages several times before you have found and corrected all the bugs. Even when the program is in use bugs may be found that were not found in testing, and you have to go through these four stages again; this is called *program maintenance*.

Designing, coding, debugging and testing a program generally take about the same time. For a program of a few instructions this may be minutes; for a program of thousands of instructions it may be weeks. This section briefly describes each of the nine stages.

DESIGN
Having decided to write a program for an application, you must decide in detail what you want the program to do. You need to do the following.
1) Sketch out what the printed reports and screen displays are to look like; what items of data you want shown, what headings there will be, and so on.
2) Hence decide what items of information the file(s) that the program is to maintain will need to contain.
3) Sketch out the format in which new data and commands to the program are to be typed, and what form the prompts should take. It's often useful if prompts remind the user what to do next.
4) Decide whether it would be simpler if the program kept all the data in one file or in several.
5) Decide whether it would be simpler to write one program or a suite of several.
6) Sketch out an instruction sheet (the *operator's instructions*) describing how to run the program; what discs to load, what to expect to have to type, and so on.
When you are designing a program for your own small business or home much of the above may be quite simple, but

having it down on paper helps to guide you when coding. These notes need only be rough; you will certainly amend them while you code, as some points prove impracticable or new ideas occur to you. Once the program is working, keep these notes safe. You may want to alter the program in the future, and without your design notes it's surprisingly hard to find your way round a program you wrote some months ago.

CODING

How you go about coding is described in chapters 6 and 7. This section will just make a few general points.

You should work out the program entirely, or almost entirely, on paper before typing it in. Certainly it can be amended in the computer; in fact you might choose to get a simplified version working first and add features later. But you should have the program substantially correct before typing. It is extremely frustrating, having typed a big program, to find a fundamental mistake that means you have to start again.

You should try to make a program as short and simple as possible. Often when looking over a string of instructions you have just written you will see that you could have made it simpler. Generally you should do so. It will make the program take less memory and less time to run, and above all will make the program easier to understand and so less likely to have bugs.

TYPING A PROGRAM IN

If your translator is a compiler or assembler you use an editor to enable you to type a program in. You type the command to load and run the editor, with a parameter that is the name you want it to give to the program file. When the editor starts running it prompts you to type, and you now type your program. The editor saves up what you type in memory. Usually you type one instruction per line, though in most languages this is a matter of choice. When you have finished you *close* the edit; you type a command that makes the editor create the file, store the program in it (called *saving* the program), and finish.

If your translator is an interpreter you load the interpreter itself and use it like an editor. But as well as a command to make it save the program there's a command to make it execute the program.

In either case once the program is in a file you can add to it or amend it at any time, using the editor or interpreter again. In fact you should never type for hours without occasionally saving the program. Until you do it is only in memory, and will disappear if anything goes wrong like a power cut; this is very annoying if hours of typing are lost.

TRANSLATING THE PROGRAM

If your translator is a compiler or assembler, then after using the editor you type the command to load and run the translator, with the name of the *source file* (the file containing the source program) as one parameter and a name for the *object file* (the file to contain the object program) as another. The translator reads through the source program and generates the equivalent object program, saving it in the object file.

It also displays or prints the source program; this is called the *compilation* (or *assembly*) *listing*. The translator checks that each instruction makes sense and is allowed in the language, and it puts an error message on the listing by any instruction that is invalid. These messages are called *compilation* (or *assembly*) *errors*. The listing may also show the machine code generated, but that's of minor importance as you don't need to understand it.

Having looked at the listing you work out what is wrong with each instruction that is flagged, that is, has an error message by it, and then you use the editor to correct the source program. You then run the translator again. Usually you go through this several times before the compilation or assembly is *clean*, or *error-free*, meaning there are no error messages.

On a big micro-computer you may have a linkage editor. To join together several object files you load and run the linkage editor, giving it as parameters the names of the files containing the object modules and the name for the output file to be produced. (Do not confuse this with having several programs that are for the same suite but really are separate programs.)

If your translator is an interpreter it checks each line of the source program as you type it. If anything is wrong it displays an error message straight away, and you can correct it straight away.

TESTING

When a program is error-free that only means the translator found nothing it couldn't translate. You now have to watch the program running to see that it really does what you intended. If you used a compiler or assembler you now load the program from the object file and run it; if you are using an interpreter you simply type the command to the interpreter to run the program. While the program is running (*at run time*, people often say), you watch the screen, look at what the program prints, type when it prompts you, and so on, seeing whether it does just what you planned when you designed it.

Almost certainly it will not. A big program that proves on its first test to have no bugs is almost unheard of; in fact it's much more likely to crash. You now start debugging, described in the next section.

When you have been several times through the process of debugging, correcting, translating and testing the program it will appear to work correctly. You should now test it more thoroughly. In response to its prompts try typing all kinds of things – correct data, incorrect data, inconsistent data, unusual combinations of data, and sheer gibberish – to see if anything can make it still go wrong.

DEBUGGING

Debugging is quite simply detective work; having seen your program go wrong you have to work out where and what the error in it must be. Sometimes it's obvious, sometimes an error may take days of careful thought to trace. The debugger may be a great help if you understand the machine code well enough to benefit.

6. Internal codes

It will help if before learning about programming you learn about how data is represented inside a computer. Earlier chapters said that on tape or disc each character is represented by a magnetic pattern, and that one character occupies one byte. This section will explain this more fully.

Each byte on tape or disc, or in memory, is a row of eight *binary digits*, or *bits*. A bit contains one number, which can only be Ø or 1. A bit on a tape or disc consists of a small patch of the surface; the direction of its magnetisation shows whether it is currently Ø or 1. In memory a bit is a tiny electronic device. When a character is transmitted from place to place inside a computer there are in fact eight parallel electrical paths (such as wires or copper tracks) each carrying a voltage representing one of the bits.

Of course in a program, even a machine code program, one refers to whole characters, or to the individual bits as numbers; one is not concerned with electronics.

A character is represented in a byte by a particular setting of the bits, or *bit pattern*, in accordance with a standard code called a *character code*. The character code used in the great majority of computers is the *American Standard Code for Information Interchange* (*ASCII*, pronounced "askey"). For example in ASCII the code for the letter B is 1000010 (ASCII uses only seven bits in each byte, the other bit being used for another purpose).

When you press a key the keyboard transmits the appropriate ASCII code along the cable to the CPU. When the CPU sends an ASCII code to the video or printer the device displays or prints the appropriate character. There are some bit patterns that don't represent characters but control the video or printer, making it scroll up, move the paper up one line, or suchlike. These patterns are called *control characters*.

Most computers can do arithmetic only on numbers in a code called *binary*. Often a program will convert numbers from ASCII to binary before doing arithmetic on them, then convert the answer back to ASCII before displaying or printing it. Thus the user is not bothered with binary numbers; nor, often, is the programmer when using a high-level language, because this conversion happens automatically. But any programmer will come across binary sometimes.

In binary each bit in a byte represents a "column" as in everyday arithmetic; but whereas in everyday arithmetic we have a units column, a tens column, a hundreds column, a thousands column and so on, in binary there is a "one" bit, a "two" bit, a "four" bit, an "eight" bit and so on. So for example the binary number 10011011 has:

1 in the	128 bit	=	128
0 in the	64 bit		
0 in the	32 bit		
1 in the	16 bit	=	16
1 in the	8 bit	=	8
0 in the	4 bit		
1 in the	2 bit	=	2
1 in the	1 bit	=	1
			‾‾‾
			155

and so it is 155 in everyday numbers. The highest binary number that can fit in one byte is of course 11111111, which is 255. Because this is so small a number it is often stored in a group of consecutive bytes; such a group is called a *word*.

The everyday way of writing numbers is properly called "decimal". In everyday speech people sometimes use this word to mean the fractional part of a number, but in fact it refers to the way all numbers are written.

A programmer often needs to write down ASCII codes and binary numbers. As they are quite long to write, a notation called *hexadecimal*, or *hex*, is used as an abbreviation. Each group of four bits is represented by one character, called a *hex digit*. The hex digits are borrowed from the decimal digits and the first few letters of the alphabet, and represent bit patterns as follows:

bit pattern	hex		bit pattern	hex
0000	0		1000	8
0001	1		1001	9
0010	2		1010	A
0011	3		1011	B
0100	4		1100	C
0101	5		1101	D
0110	6		1110	E
0111	7		1111	F

Conventions for showing whether a number is in decimal, binary or hex vary. In this book if a number is in hex it will be followed by a letter H. If a number is in binary it will be obvious from the context.

6

WHAT A PROGRAM
CONSISTS OF

1. How the CPU and memory are used

The memory of a computer consists of a large number of bytes. Whatever it might look like if you could open it up and look inside, when programming you regard it as one long row of bytes. They are numbered starting from Ø (not 1, for technical reasons); thus the first few are bytes Ø, 1, 2, 3, and so on. A byte in memory is sometimes called a *location*, and its number is its *address*. Any part of this row of bytes, however long or short, is called an *area* of memory.

Remember that to process any data a program must read it into memory. There may also be data as part of a loaded program. As in a file, any short area of memory used for storing one item of information is called a field. The actual data in a field, whether it is a number, string of characters or whatever, is called its *value*.

We have said that a machine code instruction is a number. This number has several parts. First comes the *operation code* or *op code*, which shows the CPU which operation to perform. Then come the addresses of the fields to be operated on. These fields are called the *operands* of the instruction.

In most computers the address of a field is the address of its lowest-numbered byte, usually thought of as the *left-hand end*, or *start* of the field. The op code shows the CPU how long the fields are; for example there may be one op code to add together two 1-byte-long fields, and a different one to add together two 2-byte-long fields. The length is said to be *implicit* in the op code.

In a high-level language you use English-like words instead of numbers and you can forget a great many subtle details that a machine code programmer must remember. The translator will insert them. But still most instructions consist of an operation code followed by operands, though people may not use these terms.

The computer's manual will say how many operands a particular op code needs. Most op codes need two, called the *source*, or *sending field*, and the *target*, or *receiving field*. This is because most operations combine the values of two fields in some way (for example, adding them together) and store the result in the target in place of the original value.

A CPU has in it several tiny areas, usually one or two bytes long, where data can be stored. These are the registers. They are connected to the CPU's internal wiring, and for some operations one operand at least must be in a register. The registers may have numbers, that is, addresses, but on most CPU's the register to be used is implicit in each op code. A CPU's instruction set always includes a *load* instruction to move data from a field in memory into a register, and a *store* instruction, to move data from a register to a field in memory.

A CPU also has some *special registers*, which it itself uses. One that every CPU has is a *program counter*, in which it keeps the address of the next instruction it is to execute.

If you use a high-level language you need not be aware of the registers at all. You will refer only to fields in memory. Often one statement gets translated into a string of machine code instructions and some of these may use the registers.

In most modern computers there is an area of memory set aside and called the *stack*. Often in a program you want to change the value in a register or field, but later put back the original value. The stack is a convenient place for saving the value; it is a queue of such values waiting to be used. There will be two instructions, both needing just one operand, to use it. The *push* instruction moves the value of its operand to just after one end (called the *top*) of the stack; in other words it *puts the value on* the stack. The *pop* instruction moves the value at the top of the stack to its operand, and deletes it from the stack; in other words it *takes the value off* the stack.

So the stack grows and shrinks at one end, the top. You can't refer to the other end, called the *bottom*, at all. The CPU has a special register called the *stack pointer* in which it keeps the current address of the stack top.

In some high-level languages you cannot refer to the stack, though the code the translator generates may use it.

2. Differences between machine code and assembler

In an assembly language op codes are not numbers but short strings of letters. These are designed to help you remember what each op code does, and they are called *mnemonics*. For example in many languages the mnemonic for an "add" instruction is ADD and for a "subtract" instruction is SUB.

You also have all the facilities that the assembler gives; you can type each instruction on a new line, neatly spaced so you can read it easily, and the assembler checks that each instruction makes sense.

But the main difference is explained in the next section.

3. Data in memory

When you write a program you know what items of data it will contain, or will read into memory from files. You reserve a field for each item.

If you are writing in machine code you simply choose an address for each field, leaving enough space before the next for the largest value you will want to put in it. In an assembly language you *declare* the field, that is you write a declaration in which you tell the assembler the length of the field and a name, or label, by which you will refer to the field. The assembler will allocate the field an address and put this address in the object program wherever you write the label in the source program.

As with file names, a label can usually be any string of letters and numbers you wish, up to a certain length. No two fields can have the same label. It is a good idea to give each field a label that will remind you what you intend to use it for.

While you are writing a program you inevitably find from time to time that a field needs to be longer than you have allowed for. With machine code this may mean you have to move up all the fields after it to make room. You have to go through all the instructions you have written so far, changing the addresses. This is what makes machine code impossibly

tedious. With an assembly language you simply change the
length in the field's declaration and run the assembler again.
The assembler will allocate different addresses from before,
but what might have taken you hours it can do for you in a few
minutes.

Something you write to guide the translator, such as a
declaration, is called a *directive*. A directive is often described
as an instruction to the translator, and actual program
instructions are called *executable instructions* to distinguish
them.

In an assembly language or machine code you must be
careful what code data is stored in. If you want to add two
numbers, and one is in ASCII and the other in binary, you
have to write instructions to convert the one in ASCII to
binary. In a high-level language this hardly concerns you. In
the declaration of a field in a high-level language you tell the
translator what kind of item you will store in the field; it may
be, for example, a number in binary, or a string of characters
in ASCII. This is called the *type* or *mode* of the field. In
translating the executable instructions you write, the
translator will automatically generate code to do any
necessary conversions. If you try to do anything nonsensical,
like adding two strings of characters, the translator will give
an error message.

As chapter 5 said, a field in a program written in a high-
level langauge is called a *variable*, and its name a variable-
name. This name is not a label for one end of it, but simply a
name for the variable. In many languages you needn't even
give the variable's length; the translator will work it out. In a
few languages you needn't even declare your variables; the
first time you refer to a name the translator will automatically
reserve a variable of that name. How the translator decides its
type depends on the language.

4.   Types of data

It is a pity the word "computer" emphasizes the machine's
usefulness for arithmetic; it is equally useful for processing
text. A program can work on strings of characters, rearranging
them, joining them together, splitting them into separate parts
and so on. This is called *string-processing*, and many languages
have instructions that do it.

Of the types of data mentioned in section 3 the most commonly used are:

number –   the field will hold a number
character –   the field will hold one character
string –   the field will hold a string of characters

In a high-level language each variable is of a particular type, probably equivalent to one of the above three.

A field may consist of several smaller ones. For example a field for holding the date may consist of two bytes for the day, two for the month, and four for the year. Such a field is called a *structure* or a *record* (by analogy with the records in files), and in most languages you can give the *sub-fields* names as well as giving a name to the whole structure. So you can refer both to the whole structure and to its sub-fields.

A field may be, in effect, one field repeated several times. It is called a *table* or *array* and its component fields are called *entries*. In an instruction you can refer to an entry in a table by giving the name of the table and the number of the entry. In most languages you put the entry number in brackets after the name. For illustration, imagine a string of instructions that given today's date is to work out the date a week hence. It needs a list giving the number of days in each month. You could put this list in the program as a table, with the twelve entries containing 31, 28, 31, 30, 31, 30, 31, 31, 30, 31, 30 and 31 (for the sake of the example we'll forget about leap-years). If you call this table say DAYS, then writing

DAYS(4)

in an instruction gives it the number of days in April as an operand.

You can put in the brackets, instead of a number, the name of a variable. When the instruction is executed whatever number is in that variable is the number of the entry to be used.

In most languages you can have tables of structures, tables of tables, structures with tables in, and so on in any combination. A table of tables is called *2-dimensional*, a table of 2-dimensional tables is called *3-dimensional*, and so on.

5.   Flow of control in block structured languages

In any programming language there are instructions to make the computer jump about in the program, omitting parts and repeating parts. Whether it omits a particular part, or how many times it repeats it, you can make depend on the value of some field. Thus the route the computer takes through a particular program can vary considerably on different occasions.

While a particular program or instruction is being executed it is said to *have control*. The route the computer takes through a program is called the *flow of control*. In a block-structured language the things you write in your program to influence the flow of control are designed to be straightforward and easily seen on the paper. There is only one block-structured language, Pascal, in common use on micro-computers. But as chapter 5 said, you can easily invent a simple one for making rough notes. In this section we will do so. In chapter 7 we will use it.

In the examples in this section we will generally write in lower case, because our notation is for rough notes, not for actually typing into a computer. But most block-structured languages really are typed in lower case, because they have been designed fairly recently, when computers have had lower case letters. We will put variable-names in capitals, merely for clarity.

In the examples in this section we will refer to variables called A, B, C, and so on. It is assumed that these have been declared earlier in the program. We will write statements in English, but they will correspond exactly to statements you could write in most high-level languages.

You should think of a program as made up of several kinds of building blocks. These are called *compound statements*, because you could put one wherever it makes sense to put a statement. The first kind is a *sequence*, which is simply a string of statements. You separate the statements with semi-colons and usually start each statement on a new line for further clarity. For example

        add 1 to A;
        subtract 1 from B;
        add 1 to C

is a sequence.

Often in a program you want the computer to repeat a statement over and over until some condition is satisfied. You express this with a *loop*, also called a *cycle* or *repetition*. For example

```
until A = 12
do
     add 1 to A
end
```

This means "add 1 to A repeatedly until A = 12". The words **until, do** and **end** are called *keywords*. They separate the condition from the statement and show clearly where the loop begins and ends; in a program, with a compound statement in the loop and other statements before and after the loop, you could not otherwise tell – and neither could the translator.

The keywords are printed in **bold type** or, when handwritten, are underlined, and are usually written directly under one another for clarity. The statement is usually started slightly to the right, or *indented*; this makes the keywords stand out, especially if the statement is a compound statement. The part between **until** and **do** is called the *loop control* and the part between **do** and **end** is the *body* of the loop. The condition itself is the *termination condition*.

There will be places in a program where you want the computer to do one of several things, depending on which of several conditions is true. This is called a *selection* or *IF-statement*. For example

```
if      A = B
then
        add 1 to F
elsf    C = D
then
        add 2 to F
elsf    D = E
then
        add 3 to F
else
        add 4 to F
end
```

The words **if, then, elsf, else** and **end** are the keywords. The word **elsf** means "otherwise, if" and **else** means "otherwise". As before you underline the keywords and usually put them directly under one another with the statements slightly indented.

There are many variations on loops and selections. For example you could have **while** instead of **until**, and a selection can have as many **elsf** ... **then** ... parts as you need. The variations allowed depend on the language. Chapter 7 will use some common variations.

Sometimes you have a compound statement that you will want to put in several different places in your program. Rather than write it in each place you write it separately, give it a name, and write the name in each place. It is called a *procedure* and its name is called a *procedure-name*.

Because you can put a compound statement anywhere that you can put a single, or *simple*, statement, you can write a compound statement as part of another. This is called *nesting* them. You can write any program by building it up out of sequences, loops, selections and procedures, and writing a program in this way makes it a neat and manageable job. Chapter 7 shows a convenient way of doing this.

Most block-structured languages have the instructions for affecting the flow-of-control described in the next section, as well as the facilities described here. But you should seldom need them.

6. Flow of control instructions

In other languages the flow of control is affected by individual instructions. These instructions are called *flow-of-control instructions* or *jump instructions*.

Of course when a program in a block-structured language is compiled, the compiler translates the loops, selections and procedures into the jump instructions of the machine code. And if as this book suggests you use the language of section 5 for roughing out a program, then when you write it in your actual programming language you may have to get the effect of the loops, selections and procedures by using jump instructions.

The simplest jump instruction is the *unconditional jump*. It has an op code followed by one address. To execute it the CPU simply loads this address into the program counter; thus the program carries on from this new address. In an assembly language or high-level language you write a name in front of the instruction you want to jump to, and write this name in the jump instruction. This name is called a label, even if you're using a high-level language.

In almost all high-level languages the phrase used for a jump instruction is GO TO, written in some languages as one word. A jump instruction is often called a *goto*.

A compare instruction is usually regarded as an arithmetic instruction, but it does influence the flow of control. It compares the values of its two operands and *sets* (puts a value into) a special register in the CPU, called the *condition code*, to show how they compare. For example it may set the condition code to Ø if the first operand is equal to the second, 1 if it is less and 2 if it is greater.

The second kind of jump is a *conditional jump*, which only causes a jump if the condition code has a certain value; it has a second operand to show what value the condition code must be. In other words it jumps only if a condition tested by a recent compare instruction was *true*, or satisfied.

In a high-level language the compare and conditional jump are usually combined in one statement called an *IF-statement*. For example in Cobol you can say

IF A = B ADD 1 TO C.

and if the contents of fields A and B are not equal the computer will jump around the addition of 1 to field C, omitting it. (The full stop after C shows that this IF-statement doesn't affect any following statements.)

A *call* instruction is a jump instruction that makes the CPU save the address currently in the program counter before putting the new address in its place. The CPU saves the old address on the stack. It is called the *return address*. A string of instructions jumped to by a call is called a *subroutine*, and should end with a *return* instruction, which makes the CPU load the address from the top of the stack into the program counter. So it makes control jump back to the instruction after the call and continue from there.

A subroutine is said to be *called* by a call instruction, and a call instruction is sometimes referred to as a *subroutine jump*. A subroutine is equivalent to a procedure.

You can use jump instructions freely. But programs are simpler, and many people would say more elegant, if you use jumps only to form loops, selections and cycles. A program so written is called a *structured program*.

7
CODING

1. Introduction

You have designed a program and, we will assume, you know a programming language. You now have to write the program; this is coding. At this point even an experienced programmer may feel lost. It is not clear where you should start; how to avoid writing one part in a way that makes another impossible; how to hold the overall plan in your head while working on the details.

Careful thought, trial and error, previous experience of similar programs, and generally floundering along till the confusion clears, are all inevitably involved. But over the years people have suggested various methodical ways of transforming a design into a program, which make the task far more manageable. Which of these is best is a matter of personal taste. This chapter will use *stepwise refinement*, because (despite the strange name) it seems the simplest method and once pointed out, the most obvious. The simplest way of achieving something is usually the best.

Stepwise refinement was originally suggested as a way of writing programs in a block-structured language. You write the program out in plain English, but using the flow-of-control facilities of the programming language to divide it up into sequences, selections, loops, and procedures. We will use the language we invented in chapter 6. You start by writing a very short, vague description of what the program is to do, and then you refine this step by step into greater and greater detail until each line can be turned directly into an instruction, or a short string of instructions, in the language you want to write in.

This chapter will illustrate this by going through an example. The example is from business, namely a payroll program, but writing a program is much the same whatever you use your computer for. Remembering that the aim is to show what programming is like rather than to give a complete programming course, we have kept the example to a manageable size by simplifying it in various ways (no tax!) and have assumed that you will be writing in a high-level language, so many practical details can be ignored.

In the example we will point out various practical techniques and considerations, and some common *algorithms*. This is not a computing term, but it is probably used more in computing than anywhere else. It means a way of doing something in a series of steps, so of course working out algorithms is just what programming is. For many well-known problems you can find algorithms in books, but they tend to concentrate on problems of interest to academics or system programmers; for most everyday problems you can easily work out an algorithm yourself.

Except where indicated, none of the techniques, considerations and algorithms explained in this chapter depend in any way on what programming language you use.

2. Declaring the main data areas

Imagine you want to write a report program, to read a payroll file on disc and print payslips. The file is sequential. The program is to be run weekly, on a file updated just previously by another program. There is a record for each employee, so you must print a payslip for each record. There are two types of record, because the information stored for an hourly-paid employee is different to that for one paid weekly. There is one field, which appears in both types of record, containing a character showing which type each record is.

From the design notes of the update program you know the layout of the fields in the two types of record. You have a table showing this, as below. We will assume you are using a language where a program reads a file one record at a time (rather than one field or one character), so you will want to declare a *record area*, an area of memory into which the program will put each record on reading it. You will declare the individual fields as sub-fields of this. The table includes suggested names for the record area and the fields.

Name of record area: EMPLOYEE

Record for an hourly paid employee:
(total length 29 bytes)

field name	length in bytes	type of data	contents
TYPE	1	letter in ASCII	Record type, containing "H"
NUMBER	4	number in ASCII	Personnel number
NAME	20	characters in ASCII	Employee's name
RATE	2	number in binary	Hourly rate in pence/hour
HOURS	2	number in binary	Hours worked this week

Record for a weekly paid employee:
(total length 27 bytes)

field name	length in bytes	type of data	contents
TYPE	1	letter in ASCII	Record type, containing "W"
NUMBER	4	number in ASCII	Personnel number
NAME	20	characters in ASCII	Employee's name
WAGE	2	number in binary	Weekly wage in pence

To keep the example brief we will say that is all there is; we will forget about tax information and suchlike that would be in a real file. All the money figures are in pence. In the declarations of the fields you would indicate (as you can in most high-level languages) that when the field is moving to a decimal field, a decimal point is to be put in the receiving field in front of the last two digits. Notice how short the binary fields are – in binary a field two bytes long can hold a number up to 65,535.

The first thing you do in writing the program is declare the record area and its sub-fields. You will want to refer to the field after NAME as either RATE or WAGE depending on which kind of record is currently in the area; RATE and WAGE *redefine* one another. The programming language will have ways you can express all this.

You will also have designed a layout for the payslip. Again for brevity, we will assume that all the information on each payslip is to be on one line, and that the program will be printing onto special stationery with pre-printed payslip forms, so there is no need to print headings. The information must though be spaced out to go into the right places on the form.

Name of record area: PAYSLIP

Record for any employee:
(total length 58 bytes)

field name	length in bytes	contents
PNUMBER	4	Personnel number
	5	Filler
PNAME	20	Employee's name
	5	Filler
PHOURS	3	Hours worked (blank if weekly paid)
	5	Filler
PRATE	5	Hourly rate (blank if weekly paid)
	5	Filler
PAY	6	Week's pay

The record area for the printer is often called the *print-line*. In the language you are using, each time the program sends the print-line to the printer the contents of the print-line are printed as one line on the paper, so you declare the print-line and its sub-fields so as to reflect the layout of the payslip. Here of course all the fields are in ASCII, since a printer takes each byte it is sent as an ASCII code. The numbers must be printed in decimal, with decimal points between pounds and pence.

The fields described as "filler" are for spacing; "filler" is the usual term for such a field. In many languages where you send one field at a time to the printer the fields automatically get spaced out into columns. This saves you much work, but restricts you in designing reports.

The names suggested for the fields (you will have thought up these names when sketching out this layout) all begin with P. This is so they do not duplicate the names of the fields in the record area for the disc file.

3. The body of the loop

Having declared the main data areas you can start on the program proper. First you write down the purpose of the program:

> print payslips for all employees

and then you start refining it. You can refine this to:

>**for** each employee
>**do**
>   print a payslip
>**end**

This, with the keyword **for**, is another way of writing a loop. Obviously there will be no instructions in the programming language meaning "each employee" or "print a payslip", so you refine these lines further. We will leave the loop control aside for the moment. You can refine "print a payslip" to:

> read the employee's record into EMPLOYEE:
> move the data from it into PAYSLIP;
> write PAYSLIP to the printer

This sequence is to be put in the above cycle (in place of the line "print payslip"). The file is sequential, so the first time the program reads the file it will get the first record, the second time it will get the second record, and so on. So you can change the first line in the sequence to:

> read a record from the Payroll file into EMPLOYEE.

In most programming languages there will be an instruction to do this, and one to write the print-line to the printer. But the middle line above still needs refining:

> move blanks to PAYSLIP;
> move NUMBER to PNUMBER;
> move NAME to PNAME;
> move the pay information into PAYSLIP

This is another sequence. There will almost certainly be instructions to do what the first three lines do. The first line is included in case the memory area where the print-line is contains *garbage*, data left from the previous program; any garbage in the fillers (which you won't be moving genuine data into) would appear on the payslip. But you need to refine the last line. It becomes a selection:

```
if TYPE = "H"
then
    use the "hourly-paid" information
elsf
    TYPE = "W"
then
    move WAGE to PAY
else
    give an error message
end
```

Since the record layout promised that TYPE would contain either "H" or "W" in every record, the *error check* is not really necessary; you could put just:

```
if TYPE = "H"
then
    use the "hourly-paid" information
else
    move WAGE to PAY
end
```

In general you don't need to validate data read from a file, because the program that put it there should have been thoroughly tested; whereas you should always validate data typed in, because people will always make typing mistakes. But here it is convenient to test it, and important because if this field is wrong control will go the wrong way and the program will do entirely the wrong thing. Giving an error message will alert the person using the program, so the employee's payslip can be prepared by hand and the bug investigated.

In moving WAGE to PAY you need to convert it from binary into a decimal number in ASCII. In most high-level languages you need not write anything to do this; you will have indicated in the declarations what type each field is and the conversion will happen automatically. In a machine code or assembly language you would have to write extra instructions to do it.

So the language you are using will probably contain instructions to test each condition and carry out each operation in the above selection except the first and last. You can refine the first to another sequence:

multiply HOURS by RATE and put the answer in PAY;
move HOURS to PHOURS;
move RATE to PRATE.

Now to refine the line that gives the error message. Probably the best thing to do is:

display NUMBER on the screen;
display "RECORD HAS AN INVALID RECORD TYPE" on the screen.

This will not only alert the user, but say which payslip is wrong. In most languages you can display a field on the screen

Fig. 4 (see text)

```
! Print payslips for all employees.
for each employee
do
    read a record from the payroll file into EMPLOYEE;
    move blanks to PAYSLIP;
    move NUMBER to PNUMBER;
    move NAME to PNAME;
    if TYPE = "H"
    then
        ! Use the "hourly-paid" information.
        multiply HOURS by RATE and put the answer in PAY;
        move HOURS to PHOURS;
    elsf TYPE = "W"
    then
        move WAGE to PAY
        ! The hours worked and hourly rate are left blank.
    else
        display NUMBER on the screen;
        display "RECORD HAS AN INVALID RECORD TYPE"
        on the screen
    end;
    write PAYSLIP to the printer
end
```

Fig. 4 – The payroll program so far

with just one instruction, so this needs no further refinement. You can usually write a fixed text or number in an instruction as in the second line; it is called a *literal*.

The body of the loop needs no more refining. Although we haven't yet refined the loop control we will now put together everything done so far to see how it looks (figure 4). In our invented language we will use the sign ! to indicate a comment.

Figure 4 illustrates several points. Because you indent the statements in each compound statement the depth of nesting at any point in the program is obvious at once from the amount of indentation. When you put several sequences together you generally do not bother to distinguish them by indentation. The **end** that shows the end of a loop or selection is said to *match* the **until** or **if** that begins it.

You use comments wherever you think someone reading the program will need some explanation. Often it's a good idea to use lines you wrote during the stepwise refinement. It also makes the program easier to read if you leave blank lines around some compound statements.

4. The loop control

Now to refine the loop control. It will be clearer shown in place in the loop than in isolation, but to save showing the whole loop again we will represent all but the relevant parts by a few dots.

When a sequential file is being written, after the last record, an extra record is inserted containing some technical information. It is inserted when the file is closed, and is called the *end-of-file (EOF)* record. When a program is reading the file, it can tell (in most languages) when it has reached the end because it finds the EOF record. So let us refine the loop control to:

> **until** the latest record read is the EOF record
> **do**
>   read a record from the payroll file into EMPLOYEE;
>   .
>   .
>   .
> **end**

But there is a problem. The condition is tested each time round the loop (each *iteration*) before the body of the loop is executed, so on the first time round it is tested before any record has been read. The test will certainly not work correctly; there is no telling in what way it will go wrong. It may even crash. Let us try it another way:

    do
        read a record from the PAYROLL file into
        EMPLOYEE;
        .
        .

    until the latest record is the EOF record
    end

We will write the loop this way to mean the computer is to test the termination condition after each iteration. But now when the computer reads the EOF record it will process it like any other record before recognizing it. Again the program may crash; at the very least it will print a very strange extra payslip.

This illustrates that a methodical approach to programming, however useful, will not always guide you perfectly. Only through working it out, or through experience can you know that the two possible algorithms for reading through the file sequentially are:

    read a record from the payroll file into EMPLOYEE;
    until the latest record read is the EOF record
    do
        .
        .

        read a record from the payroll file into
        EMPLOYEE;
    end
and

```
    do
        read a record from the payroll file into
        EMPLOYEE;
        if the latest record read is the EOF record
        then go to FINISH
        end;
        .
        .
        .
    end
FINISH
```

In this program there isn't much to choose. In complicated programs, with several files being read, the first of the two generally turns out to give the clearest program. Some languages though force you to do the second, because the "read" statement automatically tests whether each record is the EOF record; you write in the statement the name of the label to jump to. Here we will use the first of the two algorithms, for the purely artistic reason that a jump instruction would spoil the neatness of a program that otherwise is structured (as explained in chapter 6).

Finally we must add the "open", "close" and "stop" statements that will appear in almost any program of this type. Now the program is complete, as shown in figure 5.

Figure 5 illustrates the general shape of practically every program, other than the very simplest, ever written. First comes the *housekeeping*, or *initialisation*, in which files are opened, headings if needed are printed on the report or displayed on the screen, and the first data is read from the files. Then comes the *main loop*, in which the program does its real work: doing the same processing over and over on different sets of data, reading after each iteration the data to be processed in the next. Finally comes more housekeeping, called *closing down*, in which any running totals kept by the program during the run are printed or displayed, any final messages are printed or displayed, and the files are closed.

```
! Print payslips for all employees.
open the payroll file;
open the printer;
read a record from the payroll file into EMPLOYEE;
until the latest record read is the EOF record
do
    move blanks to PAYSLIP;
    move NUMBER to PNUMBER;
    move NAME to PNAME;
    if TYPE = "H"
    then
        ! Use the "hourly-paid" information.
        multiply HOURS by RATE and put the answer in PAY;
        move RATE TO PRATE
    elsf TYPE = "W"
    then
        move WAGE to PAY
        ! The hours worked and hourly rate are left blank.
    else
        display NUMBER on the screen;
        display "RECORD HAS AN INVALID RECORD TYPE"
        on the screen
    end;
    write PAYSLIP to the printer;
    read a record from the payroll file into EMPLOYEE
end;
close the payroll file;
close the printer;
stop
```

Figure 5 – The finished payroll program

APPENDIX

This appendix lists a few words that you may come across occasionally, but which it has not been thought worthwhile including in the text.

GLOSSARY

A

Alphanumeric	A string of characters is alphanumeric if it contains no special characters; in other words if it consists only of letters, digits and spaces.
Analogue	Storing numbers in concrete form. For example a graph, where the height of a line represents numbers, is analogue; so is a clockface, where the time is represented by how far round the hands have gone. See "digital".
Artificial intelligence	The subject of writing experimental programs that can plan ahead, make logical deductions and so on.

B

Backing store	An old term for the devices where files are kept.
Branch instruction	Another term for a jump instruction.
Bubble memory	A type of data storage device which may start to replace discs in a few years time.

MICRO-COMPUTERS

Card
(1) Punched cards are rectangles of card-board containing data encoded as patterns of holes. Although often considered old-fashioned they are still used for inputting large amounts of data to big computers. Not used at all in micro-computers.
(2) Short name for printed circuit boards (chapter 3).

Comms
Short for "communications".

Communications
The transmission of data and programs between computers.

Core
An old word for memory. Although it referred originally to a type of memory seldom used nowadays, people still occasionally use the word.

D

Databank
A term seldom heard outside fiction. Appears to mean a large amount of data stored on one computer.

Database
A file or group of files in which records have pointers to one another showing how the things they represent (for example orders, customers, suppliers) are linked together. Software to maintain databases is available only for the largest micro-computers.

Digital
Storing numbers in the form of digits. For example the everyday way of writing numbers is digital, but a graph, where the height of a line represents numbers, is not. Computers are digital machines (though there are relatively rare machines called analogue computers, which work entirely differently). See "analogue".

Directory | A file maintained on a disc by an operating system, containing the names and sizes of all the other files on the disc.

Down | (1) Turned off.
(2) Broken down.

E

EBCDIC | A character code, like ASCII but less widely used. Stands for Extended Binary-Coded-Decimal Interchange Code and is usually pronounced "ebbseedick".

Eraseable programmable ROM | A kind of ROM whose contents can be altered by taking it out of the computer and using a device called an EPROM programmer.

EPROM | Short for "eraseable programmable ROM".

To exit | Another term for "to return".

F

Floating-point | A code based on binary but suitable for storing (and doing arithmetic on) very large numbers.

Flow-chart | A diagram showing the flow of control through a program. Once widely taught and used, but not so much now methods like stepwise refinement are used.

To feed in | A term seldom used outside fiction. It appears to mean inputting data.

H

Head crash — A mishap in which the read/write head hits the surface of a disc, causing considerable damage to both.

I

Integer — A whole number, that is, one that does not include a fraction (see also "real").

Integer Basic — A dialect of Basic that can only deal with integers.

Intelligent — (1) Of a machine: having a built-in computer, usually just a CPU and memory with a program in ROM.
(2) Of a program: intelligently written, to cope properly with all eventualities.

L

Logic — (1) The structure of a program.
(2) The electronics of a computer.

Lifo queue — Another term for a stack. Lifo stands for last-in-first-out.

Line printer — A printer that prints a whole line simultaneously.

M

Machine Intelligence — Another term for artificial intelligence.

Main memory — An old term for memory.

Main store — An old term for memory.

Mass storage — Devices for storing files for direct access; in effect, disc drives.

N

Network
: A number of computers connected together so they can send data and programs to each other. Public networks are beginning to appear, which anyone can connect to via the phone; generally you have to pay a subscription.

O

Octal
: A code similar to hex, but with each group of three bits represented by one octal digit. The digits 0-7 are used as the octal digits.

OEM
: A firm that buys a product in order to incorporate it into a product of its own. For example, often a computer manufacturer is an OEM for a compiler it sells with all its machines. OEM stands for "original equipment manufacturer".

On-line
: Connected to a computer.

P

Paper tape
: Similar to punched cards, but with holes in a strip of paper tape wound on a reel. Obsolete for most purposes, and never used on micro-computers.

To power down
: To turn off.

To power up
: To turn on.

Privacy
: Making sure a computer will give confidential data only to people authorized to see it, for example by having passwords. Do not confuse with "security".

Punched card
: See "card".

R

Real | A number that may include a fraction (see "integer").

Robotics | The subject of building computer-controlled machines that can perform, learn and even plan intricate tasks.

S

Security | Making sure data will not be accidentally deleted. Taking back-ups is the usual way. Do not confuse with "privacy".

Sort | A program that sorts records in a file into a different order.

Store | (1) Another word for memory.
(2) To store data or a program means to move (copy) it to a more permanent place of storage; thus from a register to memory, or from memory to disc or tape.

T

Terminal | An extra group of peripherals, usually just a console, some way from the computer.

U

Up | (1) Turned on.
(2) In working order.

Utility | A system program that does some simple, commonly needed task.

V

Volatile | A data storage device is volatile if what is stored in it vanishes when it is turned off. RAM is volatile, but ROM, tape and disc are not.

INDEX

Computer terms and "computer" meanings of ordinary words are given in italics showing the page on which they are defined. The first reference page will be the one having the definition.

N.B. Certain very unusual words not in the index may be found in the appendix glossary.

Other Great Paperfronts

THE ELECTRONIC CALCULATOR IN BUSINESS, HOME AND SCHOOL

To many people, electronic calculators present an aura of high technological mystery. The purpose of Claude Birtwistle's brilliantly simple book is to disentangle the problems which perplex.

YOUR BUSINESS — THE RIGHT WAY TO RUN IT

Whether you are going to start your own business or buy some existing enterprise, Andrew Elliot gives away all the secrets needed to make it a success.

PUZZLES AND TEASERS FOR EVERYONE

This collection of baffling puzzles with over 120 diagrams has a unique random answer system to prevent you cheating; will tax your brain on words, numbers, logic and real life problems.

PUZZLES AND TEASERS FOR THE EASY CHAIR

Another pot-pourri of puzzles, together with random answer system (numerically consecutive answers do *not* appear next to each other) and explanations of answers.

THE CALCULATOR PUZZLE BOOK

Puzzles of all standards from easy to quite difficult to test and stretch your fingertip calculating wizardry.

Each uniform with this book

ELLIOT RIGHT WAY BOOKS, KINGSWOOD, SURREY, U.K.

OUR PUBLISHING POLICY

HOW WE CHOOSE

Our policy is to consider every deserving manuscript and we can give special editorial help where an author is an authority on his subject but an inexperienced writer. We are rigorously selective in the choice of books we publish. We set the highest standards of editorial quality and accuracy. This means that a *Paperfront* is easy to understand and delightful to read. Where illustrations are necessary to convey points of detail, these are drawn up by a subject specialist artist from our panel.

HOW WE KEEP PRICES LOW

We aim for the big seller. This enables us to order enormous print runs and achieve the lowest price for you. Unfortunately, this means that you will not find in the *Paperfront* list any titles on obscure subjects of minority interest only. These could not be printed in large enough quantities to be sold for the low price at which we offer this series. We sell almost all our *Paperfronts* at the same unit price. This saves a lot of fiddling about in our clerical departments and helps us to give you world-beating value. Under this system, the longer titles are offered at a price which we believe to be unmatched by any publisher in the world.

OUR DISTRIBUTION SYSTEM

Because of the competitive price, and the rapid turnover, *Paperfronts* are possibly the most profitable line a bookseller can handle. They are stocked by the best bookshops all over the world. It may be that your bookseller has run out of stock of a particular title. If so, he can order more from us at any time—we have a fine reputation for "same day" despatch, and we supply any order, however small (even a single copy), to any bookseller who has an account with us. We prefer you to buy from your bookseller, as this reminds him of the strong underlying public demand for *Paperfronts*. Members of the public who live in remote places, or who are housebound, or whose local bookseller is unco-operative, can order direct from us by post.

FREE

If you would like an up-to-date list of all paperfront titles currently available, send a stamped self-addressed envelope to
ELLIOT RIGHT WAY BOOKS, BRIGHTON RD.,
LOWER KINGSWOOD, SURREY, U.K.